"A lively, informative, frank, and ind[...]invaluable about the UN—and what ne[...]

Director of "Foreign Policy in F[...]

CW00969518

"From Rwanda to the Balkans to Sudan to Syria, human rights supporters and defenders have been campaigning to get the UN's members and the organization itself to reform and act on the principles it has established. *UNTold* continues Ian's remarkable work in supporting this invaluable institution while questioning its delivery—and the hypocrisy of so many member states whose adherence and support for international law and human rights is so often compromised."

**—BIANCA JAGGER**
Founder and Executive President,
Bianca Jagger Human Rights Foundation
Member of the Executive Director's Leadership Council,
Amnesty International USA

"A book on the UN that is entertaining as well as fair and accurate—and tells you what you want to know? Only one person could do it: Ian Williams, who has been the UN's jovial gadfly for a quarter of a century. Thank goodness he has!"

**—EDWARD MORTIMER**
Communications Director for UN Secretary-General
Kofi Annan, 1998–2006

"The absolutely essential companion for anyone who wants to know everything about the UN, but who never thought to ask."

**—MARK SEDDON**
Speechwriter for former SG Ban Ki-moon,
former UN Correspondent, Al Jazeera TV

"*UNtold* is a much needed exploration of the United Nations that neither mythologizes the world body nor condemns it out of hand. For those who want a critical assessment, with humor, of the UN, *UNtold* is a book they must read."

**—JODY WILLIAMS**
Nobel Peace Prize Laureate (1997)
Chair, Nobel Women's Initiative

"Ian Williams's *UNtold* is the perfect remedy for the tragic indifference to the UN. *UNtold* is a delightfully digestible history about the most important international intergovernmental agency—one which is dedicated to maintaining global peace and order."

**—CHERYL WILLS**
Author, *Die Free: A Heroic Family Tale*
Anchor, NY1 TV

# Just World Books
## Timely Books for Changing Times

Just World Books exists to expand the discourse in the United States and worldwide on issues of vital international concern. We are committed to building a more just, equitable, and peaceable world. We uphold the equality of all human persons. We aim for our books to contribute to increasing understanding across national, religious, ethnic, and racial lines; to share more broadly the reflections, analyses, and policy prescriptions of pathbreaking activists for peace; and to help to prevent war.

To learn about our existing and upcoming titles or to buy our books, visit our website:

## www.JustWorldBooks.com

Also, follow us on Facebook and Twitter!

Our recent titles include:

* *The War and Environment Reader,* ed. by Gar Smith
* *Inside the Battle of Algiers: Memoir of a Woman Freedom Fighter,* by Zohra Drif
* *Wrestling in the Daylight: A Rabbi's Path to Palestinian Solidarity,* by Brant Rosen
* *White And Black: Political Cartoons from Palestine,* by Mohammad Sabaaneh
* *No Country for Jewish Liberals,* by Larry Derfner
* *Condition Critical: Life and Death in Israel/Palestine,* by Alice Rothchild
* *The Gaza Kitchen: A Palestinian Culinary Journey,* by Laila El-Haddad and Maggie Schmitt
* *Lens on Syria: A Photographic Tour of its Ancient and Modern Culture,* by Daniel Demeter
* *Never Can I Write of Damascus: When Syria Became Our Home,* by Theresa Kubasak and Gabe Huck

# UNtold

*To "the peoples of the world"*
*who are still suffering the "scourge of war."*

# UNtold

The Real Story
of the

# UNITED NATIONS

in Peace and War

## IAN WILLIAMS

*Illustrations by* KRISHNA

Just World Books
Charlottesville, Virginia

Just World Books is an imprint of Just World Publishing, LLC

Project management and proofreading: Marissa Wold Uhrina
Typesetting: PerfecType, Nashville, TN
Cover design: theBookDesigners

Publisher's Cataloging-In-Publication Data
(Prepared by The Donohue Group, Inc.)

Names: Williams, Ian, 1949- | Krishna, 1961- illustrator.
Title: UNtold : the real story of the United Nations in peace and war / Ian Williams ; illustrations by Krishna.
Description: Charlottesville, Virginia : Just World Books, [2017]
Identifiers: ISBN 978-1-68257-089-0 | ISBN 978-1-68257-084-5 (ePub) | ISBN 978-1-68257-083-8 (PDF)
Subjects: LCSH: United Nations—History. | United Nations—Rules and practice. | United Nations—Caricatures and cartoons. | United Nations—Humor. | International organization. | LCGFT: Humor.
Classification: LCC JZ4984.6 .W55 2017 (print) | LCC JZ4984.6 (ebook) | DDC 341.23—dc23

# CONTENTS

# PREFACE

> Whatever the shortcomings of the international system, never before in human history have so few people, as a proportion of world population, died from armed conflict. It may not make headlines, but the international system, with its rules and institutions, allows states to settle most of their disputes peacefully, most of the time. Rather than disbanding it, the international system, with the United Nations at its core, needs to be strengthened.
>
> **Former Secretary-General Kofi Annan**

As 2017 began, the unanimous election of former Portuguese Prime Minister António Guterres as the United Nations' new secretary-general brought new hope to many supporters of the world body. It was a good sign that the Russian envoy to the UN proudly announced the election, which had been supported by all the members of the UN Security Council. Even many of those who felt that the time was long past for a female secretary-general were happy that Guterres's distinguished record public had already shown he was the best man for the job.

The euphoria could not last long. When Guterres took office on New Year's Day 2017, Donald Trump had just recently been elected

President of the United States. Trump's previous statements on the UN had not been hostile—after all, the UN is good for Manhattan real estate! However, his foreign policy team combined the inexperience of his nominated candidate as UN representative, Nikki Haley, with outright reflexive hostility to the UN from many of his advisors.

The United Nations might be the worst possible way to organize the world—except for all the alternatives! The UN can be slow, unresponsive, and bureaucratic, and often shoots itself in the foot. When it gets something wrong, there are lots of people who want to say so immediately. But when world politicians get into fights and find themselves up a tree, it is very often a UN ladder that lets them climb down gracefully. The UN shows how indispensable it is—but everybody else takes the credit.

OH, THANK GOD IT'S JUST YOU! I THOUGHT I'D BE FACING YET ANOTHER INTRACTABLE PROBLEM FOR THE UN...

People sometimes speak of the UN as if it were a world government. Far from it! In fact, it is the most *governed* organization in the world, bossed around by 193 national governments. Sadly, those governments often drop their insoluble problems on the UN floor and leave them to fester for decades and more while refusing to give the UN the support it needs to solve them. The UN cannot really answer back when the governments who officially own it go on to criticize its inability to solve the problems they have caused.

It makes a great scapegoat. When a diplomat parks illegally in Manhattan, it's the UN's fault. Or, when governments refuse to send troops to implement UN resolutions, guess who gets the blame. The UN is also the bogeyman for isolationists and nationalists who want to carry on killing or looting, untrammeled by international law. Often those scofflaws exaggerate, or even invent, tales of corruption and waste in the UN, just to get it off their backs. It's true that, as in any large organization, there is some corruption in the UN, but there is surprisingly little of it—not least because the organization has very little money for the size of its task.

Many of the UN's critics oppose the whole idea that underlies it: the concept of a common global interest. One such critic, John Bolton, whom President George W. Bush nominated as US Permanent Representative to the UN in 2005, had earlier said, "There's no such thing as the United Nations. If the UN secretariat building in New York lost ten stories, it wouldn't make a bit of difference." (That did not stop his desperate fight to get Senate confirmation as US representative. But he failed, anyway.)

Mostly, the rest of us, "the peoples of the world," *like* the idea of the UN looking out for us, rather than following the whims of individual governments or politicians. Every year, hundreds of thousands of visitors line up to visit the UN Building in New York, almost like pilgrims. They are moved by what the organization stands for as much as by what it does.

Those ideals move people and even influence governments. They allow the UN to harness support and get results, whether it is sending peacekeepers to end a war, medical coordination to stem an epidemic, or supplies and help to populations stricken by disasters, natural or man-made.

Yet because of those ideals, many supporters treat the UN as if it's too sacred to criticize. Such piety often makes the UN seem boring, so it's no wonder the UN bashers get a lot more public attention!

The best supporters of the UN combine their support for its principles with a healthy sense of realism and take comfort from the evidence that, bad as the state of world is, it could have been far worse! After all, without much fanfare, the UN and its agencies between them have started to create a genuinely cooperative world order.

For example, UN agencies such as the Universal Postal Union, the International Civil Aviation Organization, the International Telecommunication Union, the World Meteorological Organization, and the Intergovernmental Maritime Organization are responsible for allowing global communications on a scale that would be impossible without their coordination. We *expect* to pick up a telephone and talk to the other side of the world via satellites in space, or to stick a stamp on an envelope and have it delivered ten thousand miles away.

When a country belches pollution and greenhouse gases, it does so into everybody's air, and it pollutes everybody's seas. Toxic smog and radioactivity do not halt at border fences, so a series of UN Conventions have set international law on the use of space, Antarctica, and the oceans, and have started to deal with the effects—and causes— of climate change. The UN-sponsored Vienna Convention of 1985 that banned the use of CFCs actually saved the whole world's ozone layer!

Plagues do not need pass-ports or visas, and so organiza-tions such as the World Health Organization (WHO) and UNICEF, with its vaccination programs, have helped stop deadly diseases spreading.

UN conventions on ref-ugees, land mines, human rights, and the rights of women, children, and indigenous peo-ples set standards by which governments know they will be judged. The International Criminal Court is slowly establishing that governments that commit crimes cannot hide behind their sovereignty.

Most people around the world today are delighted that we've missed World War III so far. UN-led disarmament initiatives such as the Nuclear Test Ban treaty, the Nuclear Nonproliferation Treaty, or the ban on land mines might not all be complete successes, but they are much better than the unrestricted access to mega-lethal weaponry that existed beforehand. The UN has also done a lot to provide coun-tries in conflict with ways to resolve them using methods other than war.

The UN has improved the world in more ways than we can recount in a short book like this.

We can all (and we *will*) point to the failures of the UN, but on the whole it has to be said that the UN is good for the world, indeed indispensable. But it could be much better!

We want this book to be fun and to be scrupulously honest. We want to explain not only how the UN should work, but also how it *does* work.

We like the idea of a world organization, and we have serious reasons to doubt that national governments—even, or especially, in Washington—really always know best. So that's why we dedicate this book to "the peoples of the world," whose United Nations it should really be.

# SECTION 1:

# Simple Facts about a Complicated Organization!

| When? | 1945 |
| --- | --- |
| What? | Six primary bodies and dozens of agencies and programs |
| Where? | New York, Geneva, Nairobi, Addis Ababa, Vienna, Paris, The Hague, and many other cities |
| Who? | 193 governments |
| Why? | "To save succeeding generations from the scourge of war" |
| How? | With diplomacy, sanctions—and joint military action |

While simple questions and answers are appealing, the real world is not so simple, so we'll have to expand.

## ■ WHEN?

On June 26, 1945, in San Francisco, California, representatives of fifty-one countries who had allied to fight Germany and Japan adopted the UN Charter. They already called themselves "the United Nations," but now they were setting up the UN *Organization*. The document was so

1

precious that when it was flown to Washington, it had its own parachute, unlike Alger Hiss, the American official who carried it.

The preamble to the UN Charter is a stirring document on par with the US Declaration of Independence and the Magna Carta as a symbol of human aspiration. The lofty sentiments are not always honored, but the fact that the Charter exists, and that 193 countries have signed it, boosts all who struggle for a better life—often against the member governments who have signed it.

U Thant, the first non-European secretary general, said that "the Charter is the first, most daring code of behavior addressed to the most powerful of all institutions of the planet—armed nations."

The UN Charter opens with this:

"WE THE PEOPLES OF THE WORLD, DETERMINED to save succeeding generations from the scourge of war, which twice in our lifetime has brought untold sorrow to mankind, and to reaffirm faith in fundamental human rights, in the dignity and worth of the human person, in the equal rights of men and women and of nations large and small, and to establish conditions under which peace and justice and respect for the obligations arising from treaties and other sources of international law can be maintained, and to promote social progress and better standards of the life in larger freedom,

AND FOR THESE ENDS to practice tolerance, and live together in peace with one another as good neighbors, and to unite our strength to maintain international peace and security, and to ensure, by the acceptance of principles and the institution of methods, that armed force shall not be used, save in the common interest, and to employ international machinery for the promotion of the economic and social advancement of all peoples.

HAVE RESOLVED TO COMBINE OUR EFFORTS TO ACCOMPLISH THESE AIMS.

Accordingly, our respective Governments, through representatives assembled in the city of San Francisco, who have exhibited their full powers found to be in good and due form, have agreed to the present Charter of the United Nations, and do hereby establish an international organization to be known as the United Nations.

The United States's first African-American diplomat, Ralph Bunche, played a big role in negotiating the text of the Charter. He confided to his diary during the drafting, "There is practically no inspiration out here—every nation is dead set on looking out for its own national self-interest." Nonetheless, he soon after wrote: "The United Nations is our one great hope for a peaceful and free world."

The UN is, above all, an organization of *governments*, not people. Some of those governments are democratic, some aren't, some are humanitarian and some viciously inhumane. Most of them resent the idea of their "peoples" bypassing them to speak to the rest of the world. Lord Caradon, the British Ambassador to the UN who engineered resolution 242 on Middle East peace after the 1967 War, commented, "There is nothing wrong with the United Nations—except its governments."

# ■ WHY? 1945 AND ALL THAT

Originally, the victorious allies in World War II had called themselves the United Nations as opposed to the "Axis" powers: Germany, Italy, and Japan. It was a military alliance, but even in the darkest days of the war, people remembered the Great Crash and the Slump of the 1930s. Most policymakers knew that the punitive peace the Allies had imposed on Germany after World War I had caused great hardship for the German people and had helped to stimulate Hitler's rise to power. They were determined that if they won this new war, they would try to build a more inclusive and visionary peace.

In London, Washington, and Moscow, the future organization took shape as, in the middle of war, farsighted diplomats planned for this peace. They did a lot of declaring in the process, but it was resounding stuff.

In June 1941, even before the United States entered the war, the countries fighting against Germany and Italy met in London and declared that their purpose was to establish a "world in which, relieved of the menace of aggression, all may enjoy economic and social security."

The United States joined the war effort after Japan's attack on Pearl Harbor in December 1941. A few weeks later, diplomats from twenty-six countries met in Washington and signed the "United Nations Declaration." In November 1943, forty-four countries set up the United Nations Relief and Rehabilitation Administration to help civilian war victims, and the same month, the "Moscow Declaration" announced the formation of the United Nations Organization itself.

Behind the fancy rhetoric, the leaders were still engaged in serious old-style horse-trading. At the Yalta Conference in 1945, Winston Churchill for Britain, Franklin Roosevelt for the United States, and Joseph Stalin for the Soviet Union sat down and carved up Europe and the world between them—without waiting to ask what the locals felt about it all. Stalin agreed that the Soviets would join the United Nations, but only after Roosevelt promised a veto for the big powers.

The Second World War involved civilians more than any other previous conflict, and many of those who fought in the war were veterans of World War I, which had ended with the resounding cry "Never Again!" By 1945, they were adding, "And this time we mean it!" They wanted a more effective organization than the pre–World War II League of Nations. They wanted an organization that could stop the emergence of a new Hitler or Mussolini.

As an unforeseen bonus, they also got an organization that during the bitter years of the post–World War II Cold War provided a place where the two sides could at least continue some worthwhile communicating and problem-solving.

In the UN's early days, many Americans became enamored of the idealism and hope it represented. The first, unofficial, UN flag had four red bars symbolizing the "four freedoms" that President Roosevelt had promulgated in January 1942: the freedom of speech, freedom of religion, freedom from want, and freedom from fear. In 1944, a US Senate resolution called for this flag to be flown over towns across the whole United States: to celebrate the victory in Europe!

# ◾ WHAT?

The UN is involved in almost every aspect of human life, the air we breathe and fly in, the waters we sail on and drink. It sometimes seems it is everywhere and nowhere at the same time!

But its core is political. It is about keeping the peace. That is reflected in the UN Charter, which is accepted by every member—even if many of them were only kidding when they signed on.

Here are UN's major pieces and what they do.

## The General Assembly

Every state that's a member of the UN is in the General Assembly, where each country has just a single vote. So today Nauru, with a population of just 10,000, has the same weight as China or India, each with over 1.2 billion people!

In the beginning, the General Assembly had just fifty-five members. In 1952, U Thant (who later became secretary-general) wrote that in those early days, "The United States could usually muster a majority. It was like a one-party system functioning in the Assembly."

After 1960, the control of the Assembly by "Western" nations began to slip away. That year alone, sixteen newly independent African states and Cyprus all joined the UN, bringing its membership up to one hundred. In 2017, there are 193.

### The General Assembly's "General Debate"

Every September Heads of State, Prime Ministers, and Foreign Ministers from all around the world converge on New York. Manhattan's First Avenue is limo-jammed for weeks on end as the permanent representatives in New York from the UN's now-193 member states are joined by their bosses from back home.

The so-called "General Debate" takes up the first six weeks of each new General Assembly session. It does not really get people onto the edge of their seats except when a controversial or superstar speaker like Cuba's Fidel Castro, Palestine's Yasser Arafat, or South Africa's Nelson Mandela comes to speak.

That hasn't happened much in recent years. Mostly, the General Debate sees politicians reading for-the-record speeches with about half the enthusiasm of a waiter reciting the day's specials.

But the presence of so many decision-makers in one place offers great opportunities. Henry Kissinger once said, "I settle more problems and do more business in one week at the UN General Assembly than in three months of travel round the world." Politicians have almost every permutation of bilateral and multilateral meeting while in New York. If the UN did not exist, then something like it would have to be invented just to get all these people together.

The Assembly can vote on any subject, unless it is one that the Security Council is already dealing with. But these votes are not as momentous as they used to be. Once the "West" lost its majority in the Assembly, the United States argued that Assembly votes were no longer binding. (In an earlier era, it had been the General Assembly, not the Security Council, that had partitioned Palestine and authorized and waged the Korean War.)

However, under the Charter, the Assembly—unlike the Security Council—has no mechanism to enforce its decisions. In the Assembly, "important questions" need a two-thirds vote to pass. But the matter of whether a question is "important" is decided by a simple majority. So it seems that that designation is not itself that important!

But actual contested votes are rare. Delegates prefer to adopt resolutions "by consensus," and that allows a sense of realism to intrude into the lofty theory of "one country, one vote." If a major contributor to the UN's finances balks at something, often others will not force the issue and the precedent allows any squeaky wheel to put the brakes on forward movement. When Ban Ki-Moon ended his term as UN secretary-general in late 2016, he lambasted the growing insistence on unanimity, which he said blocked "essential action" and complained that because of it, "good ideas had been blocked," not only in the Security Council but also in the General Assembly and other parts of the UN. Was it fair, he asked, "for any one country to wield such disproportionate power and hold the world hostage over so many important issues?"

The General Assembly controls the purse strings of the organization, officially at least. It then deputes its work to six committees that have the following, stunningly mundane names:

* the First Committee—disarmament
* the Second—economic and financial matters
* the Third—social, humanitarian and cultural matters
* the Fourth—decolonization
* the Fifth—administration and budgets
* the Sixth—legal matters.

Then there is the deliciously named Advisory Committee on Administrative and Budgetary Questions, the ACABQ, whose sixteen members delve into, well, administrative and budgetary questions.

Some countries complain that the General Assembly has too many "outdated resolutions." That usually means that that country wishes the resolutions in question would just go away. For example, the United States often complains about "outdated" resolutions on Palestinian refugees. But this ignores the fact that they are still refugees after four generations.

The General Assembly has its quaint customs. For example:

* Even though modes of transport have improved a lot since 1945, and the world has become much more complicated, the General Assembly still meets for the same period of time as it did in the 1940s, when its termination was fixed by the schedule of the last steamships to get to Europe before Christmas!
* The first speaker is always Brazil, because of its part in the first Assembly. But delegates draw lots to determine which country *sits* in the first place—and then all the others follow around the hall in alphabetical order, which leads to uncomfortable pairings, like the proximity of Israel, Iran and Iraq!
* Until 1960, the General Assembly's resolutions were numbered consecutively, but they became so numerous that after that they were numbered by the session, starting anew each September.

### Treaties—Scraps of Paper?

German Chancellor Bismarck said long ago that treaties were like sausages: even if you like them sizzling on your plate you really don't want to look closely at what goes in them! The UN is a perpetual sausage grinder and treaty-making machine. Most of those treaties are essential and desirable, but it is a messy process getting almost two hundred governments and innumerable interest groups to move in the same direction.

With treaties and conventions on human rights, climate change, the environment, and similar issues, the Assembly actually does a lot of unspectacular but useful work. Many of its members feel that the Security Council is the opposite, doing a lot of spectacular but useless work, since the great powers can, and do, stop anything that threatens their interests.

The Charter decreed that, to be binding, international treaties should be deposited with the UN, which keeps a record of signatures, ratifications, and countries that withdraw their signatures. Many countries ignore their obligations under treaties, but only a few actually withdraw. For example, North Korea formally withdrew from the Nuclear Non-Proliferation Treaty, but India, Pakistan, and Israel just never bothered to sign it at all.

The US Congress sometimes gets the United States tying itself in knots. For example, President Bill Clinton signed the Rome Treaty on the International Criminal Court in 2000. But President George W. Bush, under pressure from Republicans in Congress, wanted to *unsign* it, and, to do that, the United States first had to unsign the UN Vienna Convention of 1969 which commits countries to honor all the treaties they have already signed . . .

No one is quite sure whether the United States could legally unsign the Vienna Convention, let alone the Rome Treaty, and no one in Washington really wants to explore the issue. This is called diplomatic ambiguity. It proved useful when the United States voted for Security Council resolutions that empowered the Court to take actions against other countries while it still did not formally recognize (let alone show any willingness to submit its own actions to) the court's juridical powers.

# Speech, Speech!

### The Case of the Delegate Who Didn't Talk!

In 1989, the ambassador for the tiny Himalayan kingdom of Bhutan set an example which, alas, has never been followed since. Toward the end of the "general debate" after well over a hundred very long and boring set-piece speeches, he was the last-scheduled speaker at the end of a very long day. He told the audience that since they had written copies of his speech, it would be silly to make them to listen to him read it! Some delegates claimed that if he'd run for President of the Assembly at that point, he would certainly have won!

### And the One who Did

In 2011, Indian Foreign Minister S. M. Krishna addressed the Security Council and inadvertently began reading out a speech from his Portuguese colleague which had been mistakenly left on the table in front of him. When his colleagues gently pointed out his mistake, with scarcely a blink he began again with the proper text!

### Length Records

The longest speech at the General Assembly was a marathon from Cuba's President Fidel Castro, which lasted 4 hours, 29 minutes. But the longest UN speech ever was given in the Security Council in 1957, when Indian Ambassador V. K. Krishna Menon orated for nine hours in defense of India's position on Kashmir.

## Leaders and Groupings

The General Assembly's members elect a new president annually. With the dizzying passion for rotation in the UN, each regional group takes it in turn, and the tradition has developed that each country can only take the presidency once, until all have sat in the top seat. The president, technically, outranks the secretary general. But presidents are each there for only one year while the secretary-general is there

for at least five, so there are no prizes for guessing who really calls the shots.

Each year the General Assembly also elects five temporary members for two-year terms in the Security Council. In the Security Council, those ten elected members sit alongside the "Permanent Five" founding members of the UN.

The Security Council's ten temporary members are elected "taking into account their contribution to maintaining peace as well as geographical distribution." The regional groups draw up rigid calendars of who will get what positions, including Council seats, for decades into the future!

To assure a degree of geographic diversity, Assembly delegates are divided into regional groupings for these votes. For the Security Council they elect two members each from Asia, Africa, Latin America, Eastern Europe, and the "Western European and Other Group." WEOG, as it is known, for historical reasons includes the old "White Dominions" of the British Empire: Australia, Canada, and New Zealand. Israel has also now joined WEOG because no other region wanted it. WEOG is the only group that regularly has contested election for the Security Council instead of going by rota.

Meanwhile, Eastern Europe, which used to be entirely composed of communist countries, now has a majority of members that have already joined the EU or are trying to! That gives the EU a large presence in the Assembly. At China's insistence, in 2011 the Asia Group was renamed the "Group of Asia and the Pacific Small Island Developing States." Mercifully, they allow the UN to call it the Asia-Pacific group for short.

In addition to the regional groups, there is the "Group of 77" (usually adding "plus China"), which now has over 130 members representing the developing nations. (The UN has different mathematics as well as a different language from the rest of us.) And the "Non-Aligned Movement" continues to meet even though the end of the Cold War

CLIMATE CHANGE!!...

more than twenty-five years ago means it is very unclear what this group's members are non-aligned *from*.

### AOSIS—Cooling the Assembly Down

The Alliance of Small Island States, which includes low-lying coastal states, is a rare geomorphically-based group scattered around the seven seas. With forty-four members, AOSIS was set up in 1990.

These islands have been fighting for survival since their arrival at the UN. Several of them are, after all, within splashing distance of being submerged forever. In the 2015 Paris Convention on Climate Change, AOSIS members helped to bring the target for allowed global temperature rise down to 1.5° C, from 2° C.

Sadly, however, the Paris Convention is more of an aspiration than an inspiration since there are no penalties for not meeting targets. (The islanders sometimes wonder if so many inconclusive climate-change conferences add to global warming with all the hot air they give off.)

# The Security Council

Originally the Council had eleven members, but it now has fifteen. The "Permanent Five" (P5) are the states considered in 1945 to be "great powers": Britain, China, France, the United States, and the Soviet Union (now Russia). In 1945, Soviet leader Joseph Stalin and US President Franklin D. Roosevelt both made sure that the permanent members had veto powers. For a resolution to pass at the Security Council today, it must have nine votes—and no negative votes from any of the Permanent Five. Hence, the veto.

Although the Charter says an *affirmative* vote of the five is necessary to pass a resolution, many years ago the P-5 graciously agreed among themselves that an abstention wouldn't count as a veto.

Unlike the Assembly, which starts a new session each September, the Council has been in permanent session from the beginning, so its resolutions are numbered continuously. It is a cross between a cabinet and a permanent summit meeting. The Council is the only UN body that can initiate sanctions or military action, so the media and politicians pay much more attention to it than to the General Assembly.

The Presidency of the Security Council rotates monthly in (English) alphabetical order of country names.

When delegates cast actual votes in the Security Council, they do so in public. Sometimes there is considerable on-the-record public discussion in the Council as well. But the delegates' most important deliberations are private, away from the TV cameras and public record-keepers. Even if no one actually casts a veto, the implied threat is enough to amend and water down resolutions: for example, the United States makes sure that even if a resolution about Israel gets passed, it is always watered down mightily in advance.

Under Chapter VI of the Charter, the Council can order the peaceful resolution of conflicts and even mandate sanctions against a state. Under Chapter VII, it can mandate the use of force.

There are also "Chapter Six and a Half" resolutions committing peacekeepers that lie somewhere between the two.

A Security Council decision has the full binding authority of international law, which overrides all other treaties and agreements. Council resolutions are *binding* because they are backed by a big stick. The implication is disturbing. Countries regard General Assembly and non-Chapter VII resolutions as non-binding because they don't have the threat of force behind them! Chapter VII resolutions are the UN equivalent of the Big Stick!

### The Permanent Five

The veto is resented by everyone who doesn't have one. Although it seems wrong in principle, it does have a practical justification. It has

*SG Kofi Annan and Nane Annan meet the P5!*

prevented the organization from falling apart by trying, for example, to thwart one of the big countries which, *in the real world, could not be stopped anyway.* The veto represents the reality of world power as opposed to the theory in which Nauru's vote is equal to China's.

The League of Nations, the UN's predecessor between World War I and World War II, had no effective enforcement powers, and no veto. When the League reprimanded great powers of that era such as Italy, Japan, or Germany, they just walked out, and the League fell apart. The existence of vetoes in the UN means that member states, no matter how powerful they are, stay in the UN, where at least they remain subject to the force of world public opinion and part of the world's political system.

In 1945, the veto-endowed "China" seat on the Security Council was assigned to the government of the (US-backed) "Republic of China," ROC. But in 1949 the ROC got chased off the vast Chinese mainland to the island of Taiwan, while Mao's communists took over mainland China and established the People's Republic of China (PRC) there instead. In 1972, President Nixon went to Beijing to meet Chairman Mao, and following that, the United States and its "Western" allies agreed that the China seat on the Security Council should be reassigned to the PRC.

At that point, by an unhappy coincidence, the Permanent Five states just all happened to be the same group of states that had nuclear weapons arsenals whose existence was "recognized" under the 1970 Nuclear Nonproliferation Treaty (NPT). Today, North Korea, Israel, India, and Pakistan all have nuclear arms. But these states are not "recognized" nuclear-weapons states under the NPT—and no one suggests they should have veto-wielding permanent seats on the Security Council just because they have the bomb.

The United States used to pride itself on not using the veto. The first time it did was under President Richard Nixon. They soon made up for lost time, using it dozens of times—mostly on behalf of Israel.

For his part, President Obama managed two terms of office with only two vetoes—both on behalf of Israel. Just a month before he left office, he gained a blaze of publicity for *not* vetoing Resolution 2334, which condemned Israel for building settlements in the occupied territories and for continuing to do so long after the UN said they were illegal. However, this was not a Chapter VII resolution, so there was no stick in sight, big or small!

France and Britain have been increasingly reluctant to use their veto in case it invited questions about the reality of their great power status. When the Taiwanese held the China seat, they vetoed Mongolia's application to join the UN in 1955 since although they didn't control mainland China; if they had done, they would have claimed Mongolia as part of it. The PRC has generally refrained from using its veto, preferring to abstain—except on anything to do with Taiwan. But recently it has increasingly joined a newly assertive Russia in vetoing Western proposals on, for example, Syria.

The P5 states still engage in some open horse-trading with the Council's smaller members. Before the United States and United Kingdom's invasion of Iraq in 2003, the Council also worked—sort of. The other members, both temporary and permanent, refused to agree to the invasion. The two went ahead anyway, but in a small concession to legality tried to bulldoze over forty countries into a so-called "Coalition of the Willing." (Although several of the alleged members of this coalition members denied all knowledge of signing up for it!)

But at least even the exceptionalists in Washington felt the need to have some international cover for their illegal action against Iraq. And that action could yet have consequences. Because they failed to get UN approval for their invasion of Iraq, President George W. Bush and

the United Kingdom's then-prime minister Tony Blair have the threat of war crimes trials hanging over them for waging an illegal war.

Just after the Iraq invasion, Pentagon policy advisor and Iraq War architect Richard Perle crowed that "The UN is dead, thank God!" In fact, the UN is still there, and it is Perle who has disappeared from the TV screens.

### The Secretariat: Pen-pusher Heaven?

The Secretariat is "the UN," the staff who are the continuing embodiment of this otherwise amorphous organization. Officially, the Secretary-General appoints them all. They are supposed to inform and implement the decisions of all the UN's other organs.

Trygve Lie, the Norwegian diplomat who was the UN's first real Secretary-General, had only limited ambitions for the body, writing that the Charter had created "as strong an organization as . . . could, in practice, be effective at this stage in the history of the world." The body he built up perhaps reflected his modest ambitions for it.

Some 50,000 people work directly for the Secretariat and the UN agencies. That means it has more people in its workforce than some of the micro-states have citizens.

Many people think that there are too many staff in the UN, that it's a bloated bureaucracy. To put that in perspective, though, there are three times as many lawyers in New York State alone as there are UN staff worldwide.

The Charter says that staff "shall not seek or receive instruction from any government or from any other authority external to the Organization," and pledges all Member states to "respect the exclusively international character of the responsibilities of the Secretary-General and the staff and not to seek to influence them in the discharge of their responsibilities." While stressing ability, it adds the big caveat that "due regard shall be paid to the importance of recruiting the staff on as wide a geographical basis as possible."

In fact, ever since Trygve Lie's days, the P5 governments have openly controlled the top appointments, and even lesser appointments are the subject of incessant lobbying by other ambassadors, who, regrettably, do not always have the quality of their candidates as the main consideration. The P5 lock on "their" top jobs in the UN has been weakened, but only because each incoming secretary-general has promised rival countries some high-ranking UN jobs in return for not vetoing their election. Recent secretary-generals have had the temerity to turn down particularly unsuitable candidates, but the UN is still a long way from having an independent civil service!

> If you locked a team of evil geniuses in a laboratory, they could not design a bureaucracy so maddeningly complex, requiring so much effort but in the end incapable of delivering the intended result.
> **Retiring Assistant SG Anthony Banbury, 2016**

## The Staff

UN staff are either "Professionals," who are supposed to be available for service anywhere in the world, or "General Service," who are supposed to do the clerical and manual work but often end up doing much more. The professionals are civil servants with some protection. The good news is that this protected the principled from being fired. The bad news is that it also protected the incompetent and corrupt.

With the influence of US corporate thinking, many of the younger staff are now are on short-term contracts with no protection for speaking out.

The International Civil Service Commission decides grades and pay, officially basing their rates on the highest paid civil service in the world. That used to be the US federal government. It no longer is, but it is still the benchmark because Congress would be very upset if the UN paid more than Washington.

Because UN pay rates are lower than those of some governments, those countries offer inducements for their nationals to take UN posts, even though this is against UN rules.

Most countries agreed a while back that their nationals would not be taxed on their UN salaries, but the US IRS refused to tolerate that. To ensure that US staff do not suffer from this IRS ruling, the UN pays their taxes. But then, so the United States doesn't get a better deal than other governments, the UN pays all staff an extra amount that it promptly deducts as a "Staff Assessment" and sets the money against the UN dues of the member countries. This is another US contribution to managerial "efficiency" at the UN.

> When Javier Pérez de Cuéllar, who was secretary-general from 1982 to 1991, was asked how many people worked at the UN, he paused for a while and replied, "Oh, about half!"

## Ralph Bunche 1904–71: A Good Guy at the UN

One of the most revered UN staffers was Ralph Bunche, who has a monument and park named after him just opposite the UN headquarters. A leading African-American intellectual, he had done much of the groundwork for the study of American racism that was cited in the Supreme Court's landmark 1954 *Brown v. Board of Education* ruling on school desegregation.

In World War II, Bunche was the Africa expert for the Office of Strategic Services (OSS), and he also warned about the effect of segregation when the army went overseas. (While Roosevelt was proclaiming the Four Freedoms worldwide, the US military was still segregated.)

In 1945, Bunche served on the US team at the UN Preparatory Commission meeting in London, which was led by Secretary of State Edward Stettinius. He played a big part in drafting the Charter, especially the chapters dealing with colonization and trusteeship where the United States and the European colonial powers had serious differences.

Despite being an internationally respected statesman, Bunche had to choose between working with the State Department in Washington or with the UN. In Washington, he could not have ridden at the front of a bus—while in New York he was at the helm of world events.

When it looked as if the UN would be based in Geneva, he wrote to his wife, "In many ways it would be great for all of us and especially the children—a new life, new surroundings, good schools, no ghettoes, and no Jim Crow."

Even in the UN there were problems. The first UN job application forms were copied from American government versions—and included designation for race! Bunche protested and got them changed. But in those early days, Trygve Lie even fired a young black woman who was dating a Norwegian staffer after the young man's family complained to him!

Bunche's first assignment was to the Trusteeship Council, which meant he was responsible for Palestine as a potential UN Trusteeship. Bunche drafted both partition plans that were prepared for Palestine, and he was made chief assistant to Count Folke Bernadotte, the UN's special representative to Palestine.

When later Israeli Prime Minister Yitzhak Shamir's underground organization assassinated Bernadotte in Jerusalem, Bunche replaced Bernadotte as mediator and did what everyone thought was impossible: he persuaded the Arab States and Israel to sign an armistice agreement. Trygve Lie then had to order him to accept the Nobel Peace Prize he was awarded for his work in the Middle East. (While he doubtless deserved it for effort, Bunche's modesty was possibly justified since nearly seventy years later the armistice has still not been converted into a final-status peace.)

More successfully, the armistice he negotiated for Palestine was used in 1992 as the model for a treaty between two Los Angeles street gangs, the Crips and the Bloods. Bunche also worked closely with Eleanor Roosevelt on the text of the Universal Declaration of Human Rights, which was adopted by the UN in 1948.

Bunche was a model international civil servant. He was much respected in Washington. But he also opposed, sometimes publicly, American actions such as the invasion of the Dominican Republic, Washington's longheld opposition to Beijing's admission as a UN member, and the United States's war in Vietnam about which he commented, "One does not have to be a pacifist to condemn the napalming and dropping of anti-personnel bombs from 35,000 feet above."

## UN-American?

In 1952, the anti-Soviet blacklisting frenzy led by Senator Joseph McCarthy and the House Un-American Activities Committee found its way to the US citizens on the UN staff. Under HUAC's urging, a US federal grand jury found that "an overwhelmingly large group of disloyal US citizens, many of whom are closely associated with the international communist movement," had infiltrated the UN.

By then, the FBI was fingerprinting US staff in the new UN building itself—on international territory—on behalf of the improbably named "International Employees Loyalty Board." The accused US staffers were denied passports and Trygve Lie dismissed forty of them. (Some of those fired won compensation in a decision later confirmed by the World Court, over the strong objection of Washington.)

To cover himself, Lie convened a trio of jurists who advised him that it was perfectly all right to sack UN staff who engaged in behavior regarded as "subversive" in any country. Of course, most of the UN Charter and Declaration of Human Rights were "subversive" in most countries of the world at the time, so there would have been few staff left if the rule applied.

Out of 1,760 UN staff cases that the FBI investigated in 1953, thirty-two went to a hearing. One of them was Ralph Bunche's! But during his appearance before HUAC, President Dwight Eisenhower invited him for dinner. Luckily for Bunche and the United States's diminishing reputation around the world, the committee cleared him.

In 1983, a US citizen seeking a job with the World Health Organization was told to submit to an FBI security screening. But instead, he went to court and challenged Washington's right to do that. The lower court deemed the screening illegal under the US Constitution. Washington appealed, but its appeal was unsuccessful. The checks finally stopped in 1986—over forty years after the UN Charter had forbidden national interference with UN civil servants!

US behavior gave excuses to others. For many years, China and the USSR effectively appointed and paid a pittance to their nationals who worked at the UN, appropriating their salaries and pensions. (Certainly, some of the Soviet staff worked almost openly as Moscow's spies!) After the Cold War, a court ordered the UN to pay the pensions of retired Soviet staff, even though it had handed over their pension funds to Moscow.

## The Trusteeship Council

The Trusteeship Council chamber at HQ nestles between the Security Council and the Economic and Social Council. It's a living fossil, since the Trusteeship Council hasn't had very much to do at all for many decades.

The room is now generally used for other meetings, but once a year the P5 delegates still assemble there for the briefest of token meetings.

Trusteeship took up where the League of Nations' earlier "mandate" system finished. The mandates were a compromise form of governance between President Woodrow Wilson's push for decolonization—for other countries' dependencies, if not for the ones controlled by the United States—and the attempts of Britain, Belgium, France, Japan, and others to snatch up territories from the recently defeated Germany and Turkey and to exclude American interests from those areas.

US pressure did stop the Allied governments who had just won World War I from simply annexing the colonies their armies had seized from Germany and Turkey. Instead, these lands became "mandates," with their new mandatory rulers supposed to report regularly to the League of Nations on the "progress" they had made toward self-governance.

At one point, the United States even suggested that all the European powers' colonies be converted into mandates, but the British soon stopped that. In 1945, the former League of Nations mandates were converted into UN Trusteeships.

The United States took over the Japanese mandates, called them Strategic Trust Territories, and put them under Security Council control—where Washington had a veto, of course. The islands were the sites of US nuclear tests for the next twenty years, which is not quite what the League or anyone else had meant by Trusteeship.

In 1994, the last Trust territory, the Pacific island of Palau, became independent. But dissolving the Trusteeship Council completely would involve revising the Charter, so the French suggested putting it into mothballs instead. The French worried that any change to the Charter could call into question their permanent seat on the Security Council.

### Back to the Debating Room

The Trusteeship Council may have long been in mothballs. But, somehow, many former Trusteeship territories and mandates have kept ricocheting back onto the UN agenda: Eritrea, West Papua, Namibia, Somalia, Iraq, Rwanda, and, above all, Palestine.

Palestine started as a League of Nations mandate for the British, who had taken it from the Ottoman Turks. They were supposed to make it a "national home for the Jewish people" but "without prejudicing the rights" of the land's original people, the Palestinian Arabs. But the decision ignored the principle of self-determination. The Palestinians were not consulted when their homeland was given away from under them.

It didn't work out well. During the inter-war years, if the British let Jewish refugees in, the Arabs accused them of stealing their homeland by stealth. If the British stopped Jews going to Palestine, much of the "Western" world accused them of inhumanity. The Zionists wanted a Jewish state, not a home, and the Arabs wanted their own country.

With war raging between the Zionists and the Arabs, in 1945 the British told the UN General Assembly they were giving up the mandate, and the General Assembly passed a partition plan, Resolution 181. It put large numbers of Arabs in the Jewish state, and neither state made much sense geographically.

The British Mandate of Palestine ended in 1948 in a bitter war during which hundreds of thousands of Palestinians were evicted or fled and then were not allowed back to their homes. The armistice lines were frozen with the Jewish state controlling more land than the Partition Plan had given it. Nineteen years later, Israel took the rest of the area of Mandate Palestine, along with Syria's Golan Heights and Egypt's Sinai Peninsula.

Interestingly, that General Assembly Resolution 181 on partition is cited as binding—not least by many people who now say that Assembly resolutions are not binding.

In 1948, the Assembly passed Resolution 194, which set up UNRWA to look after the Palestinian refugees. Resolution 194 stated that in the context of a final peace the refugees should be allowed to return to their homes or, if they wished, could choose compensation. As a condition for its membership the following year, Israel accepted this and other UN resolutions. But it was only kidding! Nearly seventy years later, millions of refugees from the UN's first major failure are still scattered about the world, and many of them still depend on UNRWA for health, education, and basic sustenance.

### End of Empire: Decolonization

When the UN was established, a third of the world's population lived under colonial administration. By the UN's fiftieth anniversary, almost all the former colonies were, nominally at least, in charge of their own destinies. The UN played a big role in that, albeit almost accidentally. While the UN Charter gave the Trusteeship Council a specific role in dealing with the existing trusteeships, it had little to say about decolonization. As one would expect, given that the big colonial powers of Britain and France had so much influence in drafting it . . .

Chapter 11 of the Charter contains a Declaration on Non-self-governing Territories stating that the interests of these lands'

inhabitants were "paramount" and the governments then controlling them were under a "sacred trust" to promote these inhabitants' well-being. Eight countries registered seventy-two territories with the secretary-general. Most were in the Global South. But the United States registered Alaska, which wasn't a state at the time, and Denmark registered Greenland.

It wasn't until 1960 that the General Assembly adopted a declaration on decolonization. The following year it set up the Decolonization Committee, formally known as the "Special Committee on the Situation with Regard to the Implementation of the Declaration on the Granting of Independence to Colonial Countries and Peoples." One effect of the committee's moral pressure was that France declared some of its former colonies to be part of France and therefore not subject to the committee's overview.

Most of the seventeen territories that remain on the Decolonization Committee's agenda today are very small, and some (but not all) are very reluctant to take full independence. They are:

* American Samoa
* Anguilla
* Bermuda
* British Virgin Islands
* Cayman Islands
* Falkland Islands (Malvinas)
* French Polynesia
* Gibraltar
* Guam
* New Caledonia
* Montserrat
* Pitcairn
* Saint Helena
* Tokelau
* Turks & Caicos Islands
* United States Virgin Islands
* Western Sahara

The Falklands/Malvinas and Western Sahara are the two places on this list that have seen open war in recent decades.

Territories on this list do not *have* to choose independence. They can have an act of self-determination that results in some other status. The Decolonization Committee's members are often more zealous for these territories' independence than are the citizens of the territories themselves, but there is also a reluctance to accept that the current populations of Gibraltar or the Falklands/Malvinas might have a right to self-determination.

## The Economic and Social Council

The Economic and Social Council (ECOSOC) is the Cinderella of the UN, despite having a separate chamber at the New York headquarters, alongside those for the Security and Trusteeship Councils. Instead of dealing with wars and massacres, ECOSOC's fifty-four members are supposed to deal with the mundane business of development, feeding, and culture. Maybe that's why no one hears much from it.

The Swedish designer of ECOSOC's chamber had symbolically left the ceiling unfinished—since economic and social development is a job that never ends. The UN's founders knew that the Great Crash and the Depression had played a big part in the rise of Nazism and the rush to World War II. They realized it was essential to try to avert such catastrophic economic problems at the earliest possible stage.

ECOSOC is not some kind of earth-friendly footwear.

In the UN's early years, ECOSOC had eighteen members, and in its own way it was as important as the Security Council. But many of the key functions of ECOSOC were soon taken over by the more clearly Washington-dominated World Bank and International Monetary Fund (IMF). ECOSOC's later expansion to fifty-four members diluted its actual power. It still does important if unheralded work.

## The World Court

The International Court of Justice (ICJ, also often known as the World Court), is based in The Hague in the Netherlands. It began its life as part of the League of Nations and after 1945 was revived as a part of the United Nations. Individuals can't bring cases to the World Court—and neither can they have cases brought against them there. The only cases the court can hear are between governments.

The idealists who established the ICJ hoped that its existence would make war unnecessary, but the only countries that refer cases to it have tended to be either highly principled or very weak. The strong and unprincipled states prefer to go on their own way, regardless.

Don't fight—sue!

The UN's General Assembly and Security Council vote separately for the court's fifteen judges, who always include one judge from each of the P5 countries. So there is always an American judge on the bench, even when the US government has refused to accept the court's authority!

Many international conventions refer to the Court as having the power to arbitrate disputes over their implementation. But crucially, in disputes between states, both sides need to accept the Court's jurisdiction. Normally, this works out just fine. But in 1984, the Court—with only the US judge dissenting—ordered Washington to "cease and to refrain" from the "unlawful use of force" against the government of Nicaragua when it was mining Nicaragua's harbors. The Court also ordered the United States to pay war reparations to Nicaragua. So then, the Reagan administration did withdraw—but from the Court itself, not from Nicaragua's harbors!

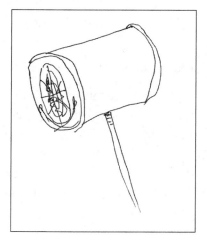

In contrast, in 1994, when the court ruled that Libya's armed forces were deployed illegally in a chunk of land that was claimed by neighboring Chad, Libya withdrew from the territory.

The Court's record has been mixed. In 1975, the Court ruled that Western Sahara was entitled to an "act of self-determination"—a point that Morocco, which has occupied it ever since, has never accepted. More successfully, in 1971, the Court delivered a landmark decision on Namibia (South West Africa) that led directly—if somewhat slowly—to Namibian independence and indirectly to the rollback of Apartheid in all of neighboring South Africa.

As well as disputes between states, the Court has ruled at the request of various plaintiff states on issues such as the legality of using nuclear weapons (mostly not, except in cases of "existential threat") and whether the Geneva Conventions apply to the Israeli-occupied West Bank and Gaza (they do). In response to a 2003 Court ruling that the security barrier/wall it was building deep inside the occupied

West Bank was illegal, Israel moved the path of some sections of the wall but continued to erect much of it inside the occupied Palestinian territory.

The ICJ has averted many potential disputes, but it needs the parties to agree that it has jurisdiction. For example, it could solve many of the territorial disputes in the China Sea, but Beijing in particular is unhappy at the prospect of its intervention.

### The International Convention on the Law of the Sea

Until the Convention on the Law of the Sea came into force in November 1994, there was little anyone could do to police the world's oceans, since they were beyond the jurisdiction of individual nation states.

The Convention had taken decades to draft as diplomats wrestled with all the various demands, not least of which was the demand by powerful business lobbies in the United States that they should be able to plunder the rich resources of the world's ocean floors at will.

By 2015, 166 countries and the European Union had signed the Convention. Many of these were landlocked countries, which were delighted that the General Assembly had declared that the oceans were the "common heritage of mankind," and not the property only of the seashore states.

The Convention made rules for solving disputes and defined how far countries could claim rights over territorial waters and the resources therein. The previous three-mile territorial limit, which had been the range of shore-based cannons that used gunpowder, was extended to twelve miles, while states could also claim an "Exclusive Economic Zone" (EEZ) for fishing, oil drilling, mining, and so on, for at least 200 miles, or out to the end of the continental shelf. However, it guaranteed free "innocent" passage for military or merchant vessels within the EEZ waters, which made the US Navy and the Pentagon unlikely supporters of Convention.

The Convention works in conjunction with various specialized UN agencies to regulate deep sea mining, and it also set up the International Tribunal on the Law of the Sea (ITLOS), based in Hamburg, to regulate disputes.

The very first case the Tribunal heard showed why it was needed. The *MV Saiga* was an oil tanker registered in Saint Vincent and the Grenadines. It was owned by Cypriots, chartered by Swiss, managed by a Scottish company, officered by Ukrainians, crewed by Senegalese, and it was at work bunkering fishing vessels in the ocean off the Republic of Guinea—whose patrol boats arrested the ship in Sierra Leonean waters. In the old days, it would have taken years to disentangle the various countries' claims and jurisdictions. Now ITLOS was there. It promptly ruled that Guinea was wrong and ordered the release of the boat.

# ■ WHERE

The UN is mostly in New York, but it's also almost everywhere else, too.

On December 10, 1945, the US Congress invited the UN to have its headquarters in the United States. On St. Valentine's Day 1946, the delegates of the first General Assembly in London finally decided to take up that offer.

With rich symbolism, the HQ was built on the site of former slaughterhouses donated by John D. Rockefeller. It raised local real estate prices considerably.

The famous Swiss-French architect Le Corbusier claimed that the design of the UN complex was his. That is contested by others, who give more credit to Brazilian architect Oscar Niemeyer and New York's own William K. Harrison.

As an economy measure, Trygve Lie lopped six floors from the plans for the building, reducing it to 550 feet. So the secretary-general's office is now on the "38th floor," a place that UN staffers use as a shorthand reference to the seat of power.

In the early days, the UN was very popular with Congress. The Senate supported the UN Charter by 89 votes to 2, and Congress agreed to provide an interest-free loan of $65 million to the UN to cover the building of the headquarters. (The last installment of the loan was repaid in 1982, by which time President Ronald Reagan had taken office.)

By the end of the twentieth century, the "modern" architecture of half a century before was showing its age. Water leaked in and asbestos leaked out, and the HQ building's carbon footprint was huge, as the walls and windows leaked energy.

Over the years that the United States had delayed payment of its UN dues, there was little money for maintenance. Finally, in 2007, the HQ staff were evacuated to nearby buildings as the structure was brought up to the twenty-first-century standards. In 2014 it was ready. (The UN Charter was still not renovated, however, and remains a little leaky!)

The eighteen acres of the United Nations complex are a sovereign enclave, not subject to US taxation or legal jurisdiction—or for that matter to any US constitutional protections.

It has its own flag and Security Service, but when the US president visits, the New York Police Department and the US Secret Service seem to take over. And it's no use claiming sanctuary in the building's lovely meditation room. Any fugitive there would promptly be handed over to city police.

As an "international" location, the UN did not accept the indoor smoking ban enacted by New York City in 2003. It waited until the General Assembly ordered its own ban in 2009. But even then, some diplomats were reported to claim immunity!

The remodeling did, however, allow the UN to clear out the cigar-size ashtrays that had been installed everywhere, even in the toilets, back in the days when smoke-filled rooms were seen as essential for diplomacy.

---

### General Assembly Expansionism

The original hall was built for 54 delegations; in 1979 it was remodeled for a maximum of 182. In 1992, they squeezed in more places for 185, and in 2015, the modernization plan included just-in-case plans for 204, although membership was then only 193!

---

## How Shall We Tell the Ways?

The signage in the UN headquarters is in English and French, which are the UN's two "working languages," though official proceedings are published in all six of the UN's "official languages." Originally, these were English, French, Russian, and Chinese, the languages of the P5 countries. Later, Spanish was added because of its wide use worldwide, especially in Latin America. Arabic was added in the 1970s. The oil states promised to pay the cost—which they did, for a while.

Batteries of interpreters translate conferences simultaneously among the six languages. Often this is not done directly. For example, the Arabic interpreter might use the English interpretation of a speech delivered in Chinese. Since 1975, there has also been a German translation service paid for by the German-speaking countries. But there is no "official" German interpretation!

The predominance of English worries the French, who have a regular meeting of francophone countries in the UN to attempt to stem the Anglo-Saxon tide. (In some of the francophone countries, such as Vietnam, French is spoken by 0.1 percent of the population, while in others like Bulgaria the Gallic connection is not only perplexing—it is perplexing in Bulgarian!)

The French supported both Kurt Waldheim and Boutros Boutros-Ghali as secretaries-general *because of their fluency in French*. In fact, as part of the deal for Boutros-Ghali's election, for some time after taking office he made half of each speech in French and the other half in English. Ban Ki-moon and Kofi Annan both took emergency lessons in French to become acceptable!

The English officially used at the UN is British English. When the organization began, it recruited from former League of Nations staff. The United States had never joined the League, so the Brits ran the Oxford English Dictionary up the UN flagpole before Webster's American-English dictionary was even on the shelf.

That's why UN people of *honour* are *recognised* as good *neighbours* whatever *colour* they are and whatever *programme* they are involved in.

By contrast, the World Bank and IMF staffers (alleged to be people without *honor* by some) are close *neighbors* of the Americans and have Structural Adjustment *Programs* that are recognized as devastating to developing nations, whatever the *color* of their people's skins.

In fact, the real language of the UN is UNspeak, a peculiar dialect used nowhere else in the world. Documents and resolutions rarely use one syllable where six will do. Sometimes it is just bad writing. Other times it is a skillful attempt to write around controversial matters without offending 190-plus member states, or to conceal that the organization has failed miserably.

George Orwell published his book *Nineteen Eighty-Four* just as the UN was starting. In it, he described Newspeak, a form of English in which "war" meant "peace," and "plenty" meant "want." It is widely suspected that this was mistaken for a textbook by some UN staff.

Orwell described the style of many UN reports perfectly: "The inflated style is itself a kind of euphemism. A mass of Latin words falls upon the facts like soft snow, blurring the outlines and covering up all the details. The great enemy of clear language is insincerity."

In the early days, Security Council resolutions addressed "questions" but possibly they suspected there were not enough answers, so since the early 1950s they have dealt with "situations" instead.

But some questions have remained unanswered for so long that they are fossilized in the UN literature. So the Council remains seized with "The Middle East situation, including the Palestinian question." And there still is no answer!

At times the UN seems to want to replace world acrimony with acronymy. There are initials for everything, not least because the system generates long-winded names for committees and operations. There is even a committee to ensure that names of peacekeeping operations have initials that spell out a pronounceable acronym with vowels in appropriate places. It is a minor art but a blessing for diplomats, the media, and bureaucrats who do not have to memorize strings of vowel-free consonants.

# ■ HOW?

## Collective Action

"There never was a good war—or a bad peace," said Benjamin Franklin in 1783. But the survivors of the two World Wars knew differently. They had seen bad peaces turn into worse wars. The appeasement of dictators in Manchuria, Abyssinia, Czechoslovakia, and Spain had led to the biggest war in history. So the UN's founders were not pacifists. They knew that strong and early military action could have stopped the dictators in their tracks and saved millions of lives. They tried to learn from the failure of the League of Nations, and they wanted the UN to get its retaliation in first, before the outbreak of a massive military conflagration. They believed in President Theodore Roosevelt's

advice, that the secret of diplomacy is to talk softly—and carry a big stick.

So along with all the rhetoric about peace, Chapter VII of the Charter gives the Council the right to call upon all members, firstly to impose sanctions against violators, and then to carry out "such action by air, sea, or land forces as may be necessary."

Article 45 says, "Members shall hold immediately available national air-force contingents for combined international enforcement action." Only a very few delegates were aware of what terrible things were slouching toward Japan right then, to be born. Within months, Hiroshima and Nagasaki evaporated into radioactive mushroom clouds. This proved that the "scourge of war" invoked by the Charter was even worse than everyone had first thought, and that it took more than signatures on a piece of paper to banish it.

The fallout from those explosions was one of the contributing factors to the falling out among the victorious Allies, especially between the Soviet Union and the others. "The UN Charter is thus a pre-atomic age document. In this sense, it was obsolete before it actually came

into force," US Secretary of State John Foster Dulles said shortly afterwards.

According to the Charter's Article 47, UN military operations should have been coordinated by a Military Staff Joint Committee composed of the Chiefs of Staffs of all the P5. This committee still meets ritually every so often, but it has played no part in UN activities. It is a *memento mori* for the hopes of 1945.

## UN Sanctions

The UN inherited sanctions as a tool from the League of Nations, where they were also not very effective. The idea was they would change a nation's behavior without the casualties and cost of war.

In the first seventy years of the UN, the Security Council established twenty-five sanctions regimes. The first UN sanctions were against the white-minority settler regime in southern Rhodesia. By a vote of 11 to 0, with four abstentions, the Security Council embargoed 90 percent of Rhodesia's exports and prohibited the sale of oil, arms, motor vehicles, or airplanes to the country.

Apartheid South Africa and its Western allies, including the United States and United Kingdom, helped Rhodesia to evade the sanctions. When South Africa in its turn was the target of UN sanctions, it bypassed the sanctions with help from Israel, Iran under the Shah, and the tacit connivance of the Western powers. In the end, though, the UN-imposed economic isolation did play a major part in ending Apartheid.

Sanctions were discredited after their lengthy application against Iraq, where they clearly harmed the people more than the regime. Over time, international support for the Iraq sanctions dwindled, but the United States and Britain tried to maintain them far beyond their original purpose. Indeed, their "success" depended almost wholly on Washington's enthusiasm for using its economic power to punish those it accused of violating them.

In 2006, Secretary-General Ban Ki-Moon outlined four elements to improve the fairness and transparency of the UN's sanctions procedures: the right to be informed; the right to be heard; the right to appeal to an effective review mechanism; and the need for periodic reviews, especially about the freezing of assets.

These days, too, sanctions are far more likely to be approved if they are targeted at individuals or groups than seeking to punish a whole people for the "crime" of having bad rulers.

# ■ WHO?

Groucho Marx once said that he wouldn't want to join any club that would have him as a member. The UN is bit like that. Although in the beginning UN members were those who joined the allies in World War II, now UN membership is open to all "peace-loving" countries, and that seems to include many countries that would prefer to have a piece of their neighbor, rather than peace *with* it.

In the early days, the West excluded from UN membership countries like Albania, Rumania, Hungary, and Bulgaria, which it regarded as puppets of Moscow. The Soviet Union in turn blocked countries like Spain (which had collaborated with the Nazis), Italy, Ireland, and some newly independent countries that it considered imperialist stooges.

In 1955, a package deal allowed them all to join, along with Austria, Finland, Ceylon, Portugal, and others. Morocco and Japan followed the next year, even though no peace treaty had been signed between the USSR and Tokyo. In 1973, East and West Germany joined simultaneously. Switzerland, although it is the home of many UN offices and institutions, was the last major state to join in 2002. Until then

Swiss voters had opposed membership in case it compromised their neutrality.

## Does Size Matter?

In 1976, when the Seychelles, with fewer than 100,000 people, applied to join, the United States was worried that as many small states became independent they would swell the Third World majority. American delegates began to hint that maybe there should be a minimum size, but this came to nothing.

For one thing, there was a precedent. The first micro-state to join had been Iceland (1946), which the allies could not object to without feeling guilty. The United Kingdom had occupied the island illegally in 1940 and used it fight off Nazi U-boats.

But when the UN acted against Iraq's invasion of Kuwait in 1990, a lot of micro-states wanted anti-annexation insurance and tried to join. President George H. W. Bush was a friend of the Prince of Liechtenstein, and with his blessing the tiny country joined the UN in 1990. It was rapidly followed by Andorra, Monaco, and San Marino, and later many small island states. The United States actually benefited since it has "Compacts of Free Association" with its former Pacific trustee territories, Palau, the Marshall Islands, and Micronesia, whose defense and

*In 1945, Stalin insisted Byelorussia and Ukraine had to be admitted as UN members. Until the USSR broke up, they never once dissented with Moscow's vote!*

budgets it is responsible for. On Middle East questions, these are often the only countries to vote with Israel and the United States!

Some small states are resolutely independent. Others' votes are up for sale. Japan's whaling has provided an aid bonanza for some islands who join the International Whaling Convention, while others have seen successful revenue potential in Taiwan's bid for its own separate UN seat. Until a recent informal truce between Taipei and Beijing, some small countries changed their recognition at will, depending on the best aid offer they could get that week!

## Almost There, but Not Quite

By the twenty-first century, membership of the UN was almost, but not quite, a qualification for sovereignty as a nation. In 2016, Palestine was an observer at the UN, where its membership was blocked by the United States, but it was accepted as a member by UNESCO, where no one has a veto.

Kosovo's UN membership is still blocked by Moscow, even though its independence from Serbia is recognized by a majority of members. Taiwan would also join in a heartbeat if it were not vetoed by Beijing.

The Cook Islands and Niue (population 1,200 and shrinking) occasionally sign treaties but have not joined the UN despite special membership rates for the tiniest states. One of their major concerns is global warming and the sea-level rise that threaten their physical survival, let alone their sovereignty, so they sign the various treaties and conventions as accepted member states.

In the Horn of Africa, the former British Somaliland seceded from Somalia and runs what some observers call the best functioning part of that chaotic country, though it gets no formal recognition from any other governments.

---

## Now You "See" It, Now You Don't: The Vatican

The Vatican is as elusive as the Holy Trinity. Officially termed "the Holy See," the Vatican has it all ways. Its unique governmental form, an absolute monarchy officially elected by the Holy Spirit, is not in itself a bar to membership.

The original postage-stamp state, the Vatican got its first toehold in the UN as a member of the Universal Postal Union (the stamp of approval you could say, if you wanted to be excommunicated). The convention is that joining any of the UN-affiliated organizations implies acceptance for full UN membership. The Vatican was accepted as a non-member observer state of the UN in 1964, giving it the opportunity to meddle in the world's love life from then on.

As an observer, the Vatican can go to intergovernmental conferences on issues such as gay rights and abortion, insisting on consensus, while as a church it tries to bring pressure on secular governments to toe the papal line on family planning. To be fair, Catholic doctrine is as strongly against the death penalty as it is against abortion and gay rights, but many conservative Catholic politicians never seem to notice that.

It has not applied for full membership, not least because it would raise questions. Lawyers say that a state should have a permanent population, which is difficult for the Vatican, where celibacy is the official policy. The Vatican has 800 people on one-fifth of a square mile: a high population density but a very low birth rate!

In Western Sahara, the Sahrawi Arab Democratic Republic is a member of the African Union and is recognized by forty-seven UN members; no members accept Morocco's claim to its territory.

In the Caucasus, local separatists in Abkhazia and South Ossetia, backed by Russia, declared independence from Georgia. In a mirror image of the West's arguments over Kosovo, Russia recognized their independence. But among the UN's other members it could only get Nicaragua, Venezuela, and Nauru to follow suit. None of these break-away states is likely to sit in the General Assembly any time soon.

## Nationalist Fission

> "A Nation is a society united by a delusion about its ancestry and by a common hatred of its neighbors."
> **W. R. Inge, Dean of St. Paul's Cathedral, London**

By the end of the twentieth century, sovereignty—and even the very concept of the nation state—was looking more threatened than it had before. In Africa, most of the "national" borders that existed in the late twentieth century had originally been drawn on maps by soldiers and diplomats from very distant European powers. They often took little account of the indigenous communities' longstanding cultural ties or economic practices. Nevertheless, the African Union (successor to the Organization of African Unity)—like the UN—has nearly always considered those colonial-era boundaries unchangeable, however little sense they made.

Ethnic differences and economic pressures challenged the identity of many of these nation states. For example, Eritrea fought a bitter, decades-long war for its independence from Ethiopia and was finally able to win its independence (and a seat at the UN) but only after a new Ethiopian government agreed to that. In 2011, South Sudan won a similarly lengthy and hard-fought war for independence from Sudan,

and when Sudan eventually agreed it became the 193rd member of the UN.

The biggest expansion of membership came in Europe at the end of the Cold War, leading Secretary-General Boutros Boutros-Ghali to lament that soon the UN might have three or four hundred members. That hasn't happened yet, but as the Soviet Union, Yugoslavia, and Czechoslovakia split up, each of the countries that resulted from those splits got its own seat at the UN table.

> "Why should I be a minority in your country, when you can be a minority in mine?"
> **A Balkan saying**

When the Soviet Union dissolved in 1991, there was a big question about who was to take over its seat on the Security Council. This was not a matter that Britain or France wanted on any official UN agenda since it could imply changing the Charter in which the "Soviet Union's" UN membership had originally been enshrined—and that might cause some people to question those parts that gave Britain and France permanent seats on the Security Council.

One suggestion was that the loose federation that was the immediate successor to the Soviet Union, the "Commonwealth of Independent States" (CIS), should take the seat formerly held by the USSR. But that would establish a precedent for the proposal European Union member Italy was making: that the EU should get a permanent seat on the Security Council and that this should *replace* the two seats held by Britain and France. The CIS anyway didn't stay in effective existence for very long.

WHAT'S IN A NAME CHANGE?...

Paris and London saw the last vestiges of their post-war status disappearing and persuaded their colleagues that there should not be any public debate or discussion of the "successor to the USSR" issue. On New Year's Eve 1991, the USSR's nameplate in the Security Council was discreetly changed to "Russian Federation." There was no official record or announcement of the change.

## What's in a Name?

For some diplomats, a rose by any other name does not smell as sweet. The strangest example of this was the admission of the former Yugoslav republic of Macedonia to the UN in 1993. The Greeks claimed they had had a franchise on the name "Macedonia" since the days of Alexander the Great and refused to countenance the UN's admission of this new upstart state to its north.

The rest of the world wanted to admit the new country as a "hands off" gesture to the Serbs. Greece's resistance led to the admission of the oddly named "Former Yugoslav Republic of Macedonia" (FYROM) instead. Over twenty years later, negotiations on the name are still stalled.

# ■ WHO PAYS?

## You do, if you are a taxpayer in a member state.

In 2016, the UN system's regular budget was about $5.4 billion for two years. The peacekeeping budget came to $8 billion that year.

New York City's budget for 2017 was $82 billion: six times the UN's if peacekeeping is included.

Most of the UN's money is raised from member states who pay based on a formula that takes a three- and six-year average of Gross Domestic Product (GDP), with adjustments for high debt and low per-capita income.

The minimum assessment for the tiniest countries is 0.001 percent of the UN's total budget, while the Least Developed Countries each pay a maximum of 0.01 percent of the total bill.

In the early years, the United States paid 49 percent of the UN's budget; and it paid it regularly, in order to shame the Soviets, who were always in arrears. American dues were adjusted downwards over the

years: to 30 percent in 1957 and now down to its present 22 percent of the core budget and 27.1415 percent for peacekeeping.

Since countries' UN dues are calculated based on an average of previous years' GDPs, countries like China pay less than their current GDP would suggest, while some rich countries like Germany and Japan pay more than some of the P5.

For peacekeeping, the costs of each operation are divided based on the same percentages. But the P5 pay 22 percent extra in return for their veto, while the rest pay on a sliding scale down to one-tenth of their "regular," core-budget assessment for the very poorest countries.

Although states can't quit the UN, officially any member more than two years in arrears on its contributions to the regular budget is not allowed to vote. Many have got very close to the limit—notably the United States, which for many years would rush its payments across just on the deadline, on New Year's Eve.

Olaf Palme, the Swedish Prime Minister, suggested in 1985 that no country should pay more than 10 percent of the budget in 1985 since the existing setup gave the United States the power of the purse. Of course, Washington resisted the proposal. It seems it's much better to grumble about paying and to continue to have the power to hold the organization for ransom.

In 1985, the US Congress cut its payments by a fifth, demanding that weighted voting be introduced—in other words, that the United States should get more votes. They complained that the UN kept voting against American wishes—often over issues involving Israel and the Middle East. (Also, until 2016, the UN would annually vote to condemn Washington's embargo on Cuba. Usually only Israel would vote with the United States!)

When the rest of the world, even close allies like Britain, all voted differently from the United States on matters like these, Congress thought it was the rest of the world marching out of step!

The UN is not allowed to borrow money. Instead, when it is owed contributions it juggles money from one account to another, robbing the peacekeeping accounts to pay salaries and so on.

In the 1990s, President Bill Clinton saw how silly it was trying to use the UN as an arm of American foreign policy while starving it of funds so it couldn't do anything. He pledged to pay the backlog. To fill the gap between what the United States was prepared to admit that it owed, and what the UN assessed, in 2000 Ted Turner, the founder of the Cable News Network, actually paid $34 million of his own money to clear the disputed arrears.

While Barack Obama was President the isolationists were too busy bashing him to worry about the UN. But as he was leaving, they kicked off again. During Obama's last weeks in office, US representative Samantha Power *abstained* on Resolution 2334, which condemned Israel for expanding settlements that the UN (and Washington) had repeatedly condemned. The resolution passed fourteen to zero. Some US legislators lost all sense of reality. One Senator called for US payments to be halted to punish the UN for passing a resolution that upset Israeli Prime Minister Benjamin Netanyahu—when not one country had opposed it! It was the bad old days again. When in doubt, blame the UN.

# SECTION 2:
# The UN's Leaders, in History and Today

## ■ THE SECRETARY-GENERAL: SECRETARY OR GENERAL?

The UN's first secretary-general, Trygve Lie, called it "the most impossible job in the world."

The second SG, Dag Hammarskjöld, said having the job was like being a "secular Pope," but without a church to back him up, adding that it was so demanding that the Charter should specify that its occupant "should have an iron constitution and should not be married." And like the pope, Hammarskjöld never did marry! It might be added that he did not even have the Pope's Swiss Guards for an army.

Another former SG, Kurt Waldheim, said, "A UN Secretary-General has no gunboats at his disposal, only his gifts of reasonable persuasion and skill in negotiation, and the moral authority of his office—where it is recognized." The P5 governments want an SG who appears to be the very soul of global rectitude and ethics, while being pragmatic and pliable enough to do what he, or she, is told. (In Waldheim's case, he had had a secret Nazi past that was known to some or all of the P5 members. That made him perhaps particularly pliable to their wishes . . .)

A more recent SG, Ban Ki-moon, soon learned what the great powers really wanted: someone to blame for the failures they had set up. He quipped that SG stands for "Scape Goat."

*"Your card says:* BE SECRETARY GENERAL FOR A DAY -- *You must keep the peace, try to end hunger and balance the UN budget without upsetting any of the member states or staff..."*

Back when President Franklin D. Roosevelt was founding the UN, he said he wanted the SG to be a "world moderator," but the vague job description in the UN Charter left a lot of room for additional interpretation. The UN website calls the SG a "diplomat and advocate, civil servant, and CEO." The Charter itself mandates the SG to be the chief administrative officer "in all meetings of the General Assembly, of the Security Council, the Economic and Social Council and the Trusteeship Council," and adds that he (or she) "shall perform other functions as are entrusted to him by these organs."

The Charter's Article 99 is the clause that raises the office above chief clerk and note-taker. It allows SGs to notify the Security Council of problems that "in their opinion may threaten the maintenance of international peace and security." Although not used enough, this power to put the Security Council on the spot means its members have to listen to him.

# ■ HOW?

The secretary-general is "appointed by the General Assembly upon the recommendation of the Security Council." That means that any of the P5 can veto candidates. There is no fixed term, but the first resolution appointing Trygve Lie said it was for five years, and that stuck. Most serve for two terms, but no one has made it to three, despite wistful hints from some hopeful incumbents.

*Mogens Lykketoft*

The Assembly decided in 1997 that "due regard should be given" to regional rotation of the candidates' national origins and to gender equality, but once again there is no absolute rule.

In 2015, the General Assembly President, speaker of the Danish Parliament Mogens Lykketoft, insisted that delegates be able to question the SG candidates, who then appeared at "town hall" meetings of staff and public around the world. Adding to the excitement was the East European group's claim that it was their turn for the job, while around the world many said it was long overdue for a woman in the job.

After months of campaigning in 2016, the Security Council conducted straw polls to winnow the list, voting to "encourage," "discourage," or abstain on their candidacies. The early secret ballots did not distinguish between veto-holders and others. Then, the first one that did resulted in victory for António Guterres, who was unanimously appointed despite being a West European male. There was remarkably little backlash since he was widely considered the best candidate.

# ■ WHO?

So, who else has been bold enough to take on the most impossible job in the world?

# Trygve Halvdan Lie, Norway (1946–1952)

> Those who gave their lives in order that we may be free, those who lost their homes, those who suffered, and still suffer, from the consequences of war have given us a sacred mandate: that is, to build a firm foundation for the peace of the world.
>
> **Trygve Lie, February 2, 1946, just after his election**

He never really became a household name, but Trygve Lie, the first official secretary-general, laid the foundations for the organization and confronted many of the questions that the UN still faces. He took office just as the global competition between the United States and the Soviet Union known as the Cold War was starting.

*Trygve Lie laid the foundations of the UN.*

The new UN had to tidy up the mess of the recently concluded, global "hot" war as well as coping with a whole new set of problems. Some of the issues Lie dealt with, such as the partitions of Palestine and Korea and the status of Kashmir, have stayed on the UN Agenda ever since.

When Lie's term finished, the Soviet Union blocked his reappointment in the Security Council, so the General Assembly "continued him in office" for another three years until he finally resigned at the end of 1952.

# Dag Hammarskjöld, Sweden (1953–1961)

> The greatest statesman of our century.
> **John F. Kennedy**

Dag Hammarskjöld was a career civil servant in Swedish Foreign Office when he was appointed after Lie's surprise resignation. Sweden was neutral, so he averted a Soviet veto, but the Chinese delegate on the Council (who represented the anti-communist Kuomintang government in Taipei) abstained because Sweden recognized the communist government in Beijing.

*Cuba's Fidel Castro meets Dag Hammarskjöld. Dag with cigar before the WHO stepped in on tobacco!*

The P5 backed him thinking he would be another plodding Scandinavian bureaucrat. Trygve Lie opposed his nomination because he judged he would be "no more than a clerk." (That probably helped persuade the Security Council to give him the job!)

In office, Hammarskjöld was willing to defy the great powers. He announced that he welcomed "the final, least tangible, but perhaps most important new factor in diplomacy: mass public opinion as a living force in international affairs." An SG, he thought, had to use his pulpit to reach beyond the politicians with the UN agenda. He was an equal-opportunity irritant, annoying East and West alike.

## Meditation Room

As well as taking deep interest in the UN's growing art collection, Hammarskjöld commissioned the creation of the Meditation Room, a non-denominational place for quiet contemplation in the General Assembly building. It is certainly quiet. A French Ambassador listed it as one of the best places to take a nap in UNHQ!

When Soviet premier Nikita Khrushchev called for his resignation, Hammarskjöld's reply brought a standing ovation in the Assembly. "It is very easy to resign; it is not so easy to stay on. It is very easy to bow to the wish of a big power. It is another matter to resist.... I have done so before on many occasions and in many directions. If it is the wish of those nations who see in the Organization their best protection in the present world, I shall now do so again." It was. He stayed.

In 1961, the UN tried to implement its own resolutions on the Congo. This time, it was the White House that was opposed. Hammarskjöld notably wrote, "It is better for the UN to lose the support of the US because it is faithful to law and principles than to survive as an agent whose activities are geared to political purposes never avowed or laid down by the major organs of the UN."

It was dangerous upsetting the West. In 1961, his plane crashed between the Congo and what is now Zambia, killing Hammarskjöld and taking down with it many of the hopes of the UN. In 2016, Ban Ki-moon announced a new Inquiry into the crash.

## U Thant, Burma (1961–1971)

Hammarskjöld had named U Thant as a possible successor, and the Council concurred. A devout Buddhist, the former Burmese

*U Thant points the way.*

representative to the UN was also an astrologer, claiming that the movements of Saturn foretold US President Johnson's decision to step down in 1968. But even if he had his eyes to the heavens, his feet were on the ground. "When I am equally criticized by the US and the USSR, I know that I am right," he said. That is not a bad rule of thumb for the job!

These even more prescient words of his have rung down through the decades: "This widening gap in economic progress between the wealthy and the poor (is) ultimately more explosive than political or ideological differences."

People might have complained about U Thant's low profile in life, but after he died in 1974, ordinary Burmese took to the streets to commemorate him, and there were riots when Burma's military junta tried to ignore his funeral.

# Kurt Waldheim, Austria (1972–1981)

## *World Leader or War Criminal?*

In 1972, *Oberleutnant* Kurt Waldheim, a former Nazi party member and suspected war criminal, became head of the organization that

was originally set up to defeat the German army he had fought for. Maybe this was why Irish writer Conor Cruise O'Brien said that Waldheim had "exactly the combination of qualities which the super-powers agree in regarding as desirable in a Secretary-General"?

US submissions to the UN's own War Crimes Commission in 1948 had listed Waldheim as a highest category suspect for his role in the Balkans. A year later, the Commission's archives were closed to the public, and it was not until 2012 that Ban Ki-moon made them public.

Brian Urquhart, the urbane British diplomat who had been a senior UN staff member since 1945, said Waldheim was at one and the same time "a scheming ambitious, duplicitous egomaniac ready to do anything for advantage or public acclaim," and "a statesman-like leader who kept his head while all about him were losing theirs." In 1981, the Chinese nixed his try for third term saying they wanted a Third World candidate.

Waldheim's dubious war record only emerged after his retirement, when he ran for President of Austria. By then, the US government had decided to bar him from visiting so he could not return to New York for the UN's fiftieth anniversary celebrations in 1995. (On the other hand, the Pope knighted him.)

# Javier Pérez de Cuéllar, Peru (1982–1991)

### The Invisible Man?

To satisfy the Chinese, the United States put up this Peruvian aristocrat as the developing-world candidate. On becoming SG, Pérez de Cuéllar sacked UN Human Rights director Theo Van Boven after Jeane Kirkpatrick, President Ronald Reagan's Ambassador to the UN, pressured him to. The Iraqis invaded Kuwait in his last year as SG. According to the Iraqis and others, under heavy US pressure, Pérez de Cuéllar suppressed peace overtures that Iraq had launched to try to stave off US-led military action. The White House wanted a quick and successful war.

As he finished his term in 1991, his last act over the end-of-year holidays was to try to spring a deal on the Council that would have given King Hassan of Morocco almost everything he wanted in the long-contested Western Sahara. He was unsuccessful, but the Moroccans offered him a lucrative directorship in a company they owned in France anyway.

## Boutros Boutros-Ghali, Egypt (1992–1996)

African countries insisted it was Africa's turn, but they could not agree on which African! So, the French proposed Boutros Boutros-Ghali, a Coptic Christian aristocrat and acting Egyptian foreign minister. Nominally African, French speaking, and from an Arab country, he ticked some boxes for everyone.

He genuinely demanded attention for Africa, a continent that

Washington had long overlooked. During the Balkan Wars, he said, "Genocide in Africa has not received the same attention that genocide in Europe or genocide in Turkey or genocide in other parts of the world [had]. There is still this kind of basic discrimination against the African people and the African problems."

When he landed in besieged and starving Sarajevo, telling its residents there were ten places in the world worse off than them may have been truthful . . . but it was not very tactful.

He had one particular target for his criticisms: the United States. In 1996, President Clinton's Ambassador to the UN, Madeleine Albright, vetoed the vote the Security Council's fourteen other members had cast, to give him another term. (That veto lubricated Albright's path to confirmation as Secretary of State, averting opposition from the powerful Chair of the Senate Foreign Relations committee, Jesse Helms, who was an enemy of the UN in general but particularly of Boutros-Ghali.)

In the memoir he published in 1999, Boutros-Ghali wrote:

> When the United Nations was allowed to do its job without substantial US involvement, as in Mozambique, the operation succeeded. When the United States felt a political need for the United Nations, as in Haiti, the operation also fulfilled its main objective. But when the United States wanted to appear actively involved, while in reality avoiding hard decisions, as in Bosnia, Somalia, and Rwanda, the United Nations was misused, abused, or blamed by the United States and the operations failed, tragically, and horribly.

# Kofi Annan, Ghana (1997–2006)

### The Insider

The first SG to come up through the ranks of the UN, Kofi Annan was the Clinton administration's response to the African states' insistence that it was still "their turn." To keep Washington happy, Annan balanced UN "reforms" with aid and trade concessions for the developing world. He even got the United States to pay its dues ... and he persuaded President George W. Bush to sign on to the Millennium Development Goals (MDGs) adopted at a World Summit in 2000, which was the largest gathering of government leaders ever. The MDGs committed the world to tackling poverty and under-development by defining a series of targets that should be met within fifteen years. In 2001, Annan won the Nobel Peace Prize.

Another major achievement was the *Responsibility to Protect* (R2P), a policy that defined the parameters for "humanitarian interventions" in response to in-country atrocities; Annan steered this through another World Summit of heads of government in 2005.

Less successfully, but still an improvement, he also managed the replacement of the Human Rights Commission by the Human Rights Council.

Annan was well aware of the limited powers of his office. "You can do a lot with diplomacy, but with diplomacy backed up by force you can get a lot more done," he once commented wryly after an occasion on which he persuaded Iraqi leader Saddam Hussein to step back from the brink. But, of course, it is not often that an SG has even the hint of force to back him up.

Pressed by a BBC reporter in 2004, Annan admitted that the US-led 2003 invasion of Iraq was illegal. Even that belated and low-key criticism of Washington brought down the wrath of the right-wingers in the United States, who then went on to invent the Oil for Food "Scandal."

# Ban Ki-moon, Republic of Korea (2007–2016)

### The Scape Goat?

Ban Ki-moon was South Korean Foreign Minister when he was elected. The P5 probably agreed to him because his low-key oratorical delivery and diplomacy had lured them into thinking that he was their ideal candidate—more secretary than general. He was Asian, which is what the Chinese wanted, and the United States thought he was safe as foreign minister of an allied country, even though during his election campaign he enthusiastically supported the International Criminal Court that US Representative John Bolton had been trying to destroy.

# Oil for Food

After the Gulf War of 1991, the United States had rammed through the Security Council the "Mother of All Resolutions," which imposed harsh sanctions on Iraq over its suspected stock of "Weapons of Mass Destruction" (WMDs). The mass poverty and malnutrition that these inflicted on Iraq led most Security Council members to want to lift or soften the sanctions, but the West threatened to veto any resolution that would do this. Human rights groups reported that the sanctions had killed 500,000 children—but US ambassador Madeleine Albright still said this was a price was worth paying. (Saddam and his cronies, meanwhile, found numerous ways to evade, and even profit from, the sanctions.)

In 1995, the widespread reluctance to maintain the sanctions led to the *Oil for Food* program, under which Iraq was allowed to sell oil, but the UN banked the proceeds to pay for food and other essentials agreed by a Security Council sanctions committee.

In the mid-aughts, the anti-UN media in the United States mounted a campaign against the UN for the alleged corruption in the Oil for Food program (which had ended when the US-led coalition invaded Iraq in 2003). Their real target was Annan for having said that the war had been illegal. The *Wall Street Journal* called the program "the largest fraud ever recorded in history." On Fox News, it was described as the "biggest scandal in human history." After years of shrill headlines, however, the only substantial allegation left standing was that one UN official had a suspicious $150,000 in his bank account.

There was a lot less fuss from these media later when it was revealed that Washington could not account for some $10 billion of the Oil For Food cash it took for "rebuilding" Iraq after the US-led invasion of 2003.

Annan described the attacks on him and on the UN as "a bit like a lynching." The media had conjured up large clouds of smoke from a very small fire. Now that the 2003 invasion is more widely accepted as having been a disaster, the so-called scandal is almost completely forgotten, and it no longer threatens his reputation—or the UN's.

Perhaps because President George W. Bush supported Ban, the Republicans never attacked him despite his strong advocacy for the UN system.

Ban was proud of his work on issues such as gender, disarmament, and climate change, which he made a particular concern, and in his final year he launched the Sustainable Development Goals. Also, as he left office at the end of 2016, he expressed an outspoken opinion about Israel's settlement activity in the occupied territories, describing it as "in flagrant violation of international law and the Fourth Geneva Convention."

## António Guterres, Portugal (2017– )

### A New Broom?

A former Prime Minister of Portugal, Guterres was the first former head of government to become SG. He had also been President of the Socialist International and then UN High Commissioner for Refugees, so he was familiar with the UN's workings and was a respected international figure.

He also seemed to have the "vision thing." In the run-up

to the election, he told *Time* magazine that "the ability to be an advocate for our true universal values is essential in the Secretary-General's job to strengthen the UN and ensure its centrality and peoples' trust."

In an organization with many jaundiced and cynical observers, Guterres had an unusually warm reception, but he did not let it go to his head. Just after being elected he said modestly,

> I know the Secretary-General is not the leader of the world. I know that the role of the Secretary-General is just to be conceived as an added value. The primacy of the work comes to Member States. But I will be there to support all Member States that, using goodwill, understand that now it's time to bring those conflicts to an end.

## The Deputies!

Another Kofi Annan innovation was to get Assembly approval for a Deputy Secretary-General. This position is not mentioned not in the Charter, and the secretary-general appoints her or him. The deputy is often a woman, to make up for the lack of a woman in the top seat. The following people have taken on this job:

**Louise Frechette**, March 1998–March 2006. Frechette, a Canadian, was the former prosecutor of the International Tribunal for the former Yugoslavia. She was appointed by Kofi Annan.

**Mark Malloch Brown**, March-December 2006. Malloch Brown, a Briton, had been the first non-US head of UN Development Program (UNDP) and was highly outspoken about US attitudes to the UN during the Iraq War. He was also appointed by Kofi Annan.

**Dr. Asha-Rose Migiro,** 2007–2012. Migiro, a Tanzanian, was appointed by Ban Ki-moon.

**Jan Eliasson**, 2012–2016. Eliasson, from Sweden, had held many posts in the UN's Department of Humanitarian Affairs. He was appointed by Ban Ki-moon.

**Amina Mohamed,** 2017– . Mohamed had been Nigeria's Environment Minister, and was Guterres's first appointment.

# That Scourge of War Thing—Peace and Disarmament

## ■ THE UN IN UNIFORM

> Boutros-Ghali once said despairingly, "I can do nothing. I have no army. I have no money. I have no experts. I am borrowing everything. If the member states don't want it, what can I do?" But he also noted that, when big countries do want something, they can miraculously find the means to get it.

### Korea: The UN's First War!

Toward the end of World War II, the Soviets and the United States had liberated Korea from the Japanese, and each occupied half of it.

In 1947, the General Assembly set up a commission to hold elections and oversee the withdrawal of occupying troops from Korea. The Soviets did not allow the commission to enter their half, let alone hold elections, so in 1948 the commission and the General Assembly recognized the South Korean government.

From January through August of 1950, the Soviet Union boycotted the Security Council—to protest Washington's veto of the communist government in Beijing holding China's seat on the Security Council. Moscow's timing for the boycott was terrible. With the Soviet Ambassador absent, the Council declared the North the aggressor when it invaded and asked members to send troops to support South Korea under the "Unified Command" of the US military, authorizing their use of the UN flag.

Even now, the UN flag flies over the Panmunjom border crossing between North and South Korea, and the troops on the Southern side are techni-

*Troops under the UN flag in Korea, but Lie was their Secretary, not their General!*

cally the UN Command Security Battalion. Even now, there is only an armistice in Korea but no peace treaty, since the North, the Democratic People's Republic of Korea, is still at war with the UN—of which it is now also a member!

Once the Soviets returned to the Security Council, the West shifted deliberations on Korea to the General Assembly, where Moscow had no veto. At US urging, the UN changed the rules so that seven members of the Security Council or

the majority of the Assembly members could call an emergency session. If the Council was deadlocked by a veto, the Assembly could call upon UN members to act under a special provision called a "Uniting for Peace" resolution.

Ironically, the first time the Uniting For Peace provision was used, in 1956, it was as part of a joint US-Soviet move to condemn the British/French/Israeli attack on Egypt. (Britain and France had vetoed a Security Council resolution condemning the attack.) Then, in the 1960s, when the West lost its majority in the General Assembly, US enthusiasm for the "Uniting for Peace" procedure diminished greatly.

In the 1990s, the Palestinian delegation rediscovered the procedure and used it to bypass the US veto for Israel in the Security Council—whereupon the United States, which had invented the procedure, denied its legitimacy.

## The First Blue Helmets

Peacekeeping missions undertaken by the UN are a different thing than the fighting that took place under its flag in Korea. The UN's first-ever peacekeeping mission was the UN Truce Supervision Organization (UNTSO), which was established in May 1948 to keep the peace between Israel and the Arab states bordering it. UNTSO is still around today and Israel still does not have peace with Syria, Lebanon, or the Palestinians.

In 1949, the United Nations Military Observer Group in India and Pakistan (UNMOGIP) was deployed to monitor the cease-fire along the Line of Control between India and Pakistan in Kashmir, a region whose status is still contested today.

The modern concept of peacekeepers with distinctive blue helmets and white vehicles began in 1956, after France, Israel, and Britain attacked Egypt. Times were different then. When Israel refused to withdraw from Egypt, President Dwight Eisenhower asked, "Should a nation which attacks and occupies foreign territory in the face of United Nations disapproval be allowed to impose conditions on its own withdrawal? If we agree that an armed attack can properly achieve

*The Danish contingent for UNEF, the first peacekeepers.*

the purposes of the assailant, then I fear we will have turned back the clock of international order."

In 1956, Canadian Prime Minister Lester Pearson proposed to monitor the UN-ordered cease-fire in Egypt's Sinai region with "a truly international peace and police force . . . large enough to keep these borders at peace while a political settlement is being worked out." The Assembly agreed and UNEF, the UN Emergency Force, was born.

US clout forced Britain, France, and eventually Israel to agree to UNEF's deployment. Its troops came from Brazil, Canada, Ceylon, Colombia, Norway, India, and Yugoslavia. Many of them wore uniforms similar to the invading British

*Lester Pearson, Canadian Nobel winner and UN peacemaker after Suez.*

*Don't it make your green hats blue? Danes before and after the blue painted helmets!*

troops, so they were given the distinctive UN-blue berets to avoid confusion.

But there always seemed to be more emergencies, so the UN-blue headgear—berets or helmets—became a semi-permanent feature of the world's crisis zones.

When the Israeli attack started on June 5, fourteen UNEF soldiers were killed. Israel occupied the Golan Heights, the West Bank (including East Jerusalem), the Gaza Strip, and the Sinai Peninsula right up to the Suez Canal. This time, there was no Eisenhower in the White House to apply pressure, either directly or through the UN. And Israel's military occupation of the West Bank and Golan Heights continues today.

# UNchartered Course for Peacekeeping

The UN Charter never mentions peacekeeping, so the UN's Department of Peacekeeping Operations (DPKO) has

## Withdrawal of Peacekeepers Triggers War

UNEF's deployment in 1956 allowed everyone to climb down gracefully. The Israelis and the Egyptians denounced it in public while privately accepting its presence with a sigh of relief, although Israel refused to accept NEF troops on its side of the border. The Soviets and French refused to accept peacekeeping's legitimacy and so wouldn't pay for it. Even so, UNEF kept the peace for ten years.

When tensions rose in 1967, Egypt's President Gamal Abdel-Nasser asked for the peacekeepers to be taken out. UN Secretary-General U Thant was widely attacked when he complied, though legally he had no option. Indeed, two of the force's largest contingents, the Indians and Yugoslavs, refused to stay if Egypt wanted them out, and Israel rebuffed a suggestion that UNEF be redeployed to their side of the line. In the meantime, the Egyptian Army had moved up to the border, which meant UNEF was no longer a buffer force.

Egypt was publicly bellicose but privately scared of war, while Israel publicly expressed worry but privately looked forward to another war.

had to make up its own guidelines as it goes along. Insiders sometimes refer to its job as Chapter Six-and-a-Half, falling somewhere between the scope of the Charter's Chapters Six (peaceful means) and Seven (forceful means.)

For many years, peacekeepers have been the UNs icons: "soldiers for peace"! In 1989, they won the Nobel Peace Prize. Instead of the founders' original idea, that the Big Five would stomp on any trouble-makers, for years the UN would not use troops from the P5, nor from former colonial powers or rival neighbors.

In the early 1990s, the end of the Cold War made peacekeeping operations bigger and more complex, and the UN had to start to accept troops from whichever country was willing to provide them. Some national contingents are so pacifist or hyper-neutral that when a faction stops them at a barricade they will hand over their weapons. Others make it plain that there will be robust consequences. By 2016, there were over 100,000 UN peacekeepers deployed in 16 different missions around the world.

The blue headgear and the white UN vehicles are supposed to show that peacekeepers aren't part of the conflict, but if one side is committing criminal acts it makes UN forces seem accomplices if they treat the perpetrators and their victims equally in the name of impartiality and neutrality.

Peacekeeping forces and observers can deter barbaric behavior, but only if the perpetrators are convinced that retribution could follow. Otherwise they are just a blue fig leaf to cover the inaction of the major powers.

Too often, Security Council members want to be *seen* to be doing something, and they authorize operations while refusing to provide enough troops to make the operations effective. In Bosnia and Rwanda, the Council effectively abandoned peacekeepers and thousands of civilians were murdered.

When peacekeepers were attacked in Bosnia in the mid-1990s, a British general commented, "You don't go to war in white tanks." At his recommendation, eventually peacekeepers in the Balkans were equipped with artillery and backed by airplanes—and they used them, too.

## Never Ending Stories—UN Operations That Last!

*Congo*

The UN was involved in Congo for the first time from 1960 to 1964. More than fifty years later, it's still there.

When Congo won its independence from Belgium in 1960, in the whole massive country there was not a single Congolese military officer and only sixteen university graduates. After independence, the troops saw no reason to continue to obey their Belgian officers. Mutinies and secessions, often fomented by outside powers, caused chaos, especially in the mineral rich province of Katanga.

The first Prime Minister, Patrice Lumumba, asked the UN for help, and Dag Hammarskjöld used the secretary-general's powers under Article 99 to put the matter on the Security Council agenda. The Council authorized a whole new force, the United Nations Operation in Congo (ONUC), to go to Congo's help.

Before long though, Lumumba was deposed, handed over to the Katangese secessionists, and murdered (probably with the connivance of the Belgians and the CIA).

Congo has never recovered from its chaotic birth. Now known as the Democratic Republic of Congo (DRC), it has been in chaos for half a century and now hosts one of

*Dag Hammarskjöld greets Patrice Lumbumba, the short-lived first President of Congo. Hammarskjöld did not long outlive him.*

the biggest UN forces, now named MONUC. The country has had to contend with weak but rapacious governments and innumerable militias sponsored by neighbors, all eager to get their hands on the country's minerals. The UN force, for all its problems, helps to keeps Congo together.

### Cyprus, The Island of Aphrodite, Goddess of Love

In 1960, the British granted independence to Cyprus, whose government was supposed to represent both the island's Greek majority and its Turkish minority.

When the two communities instead split the island between them, the British passed the buck to the UN. Ralph Bunche, who had experience in the region, warned, "If you go in there, you'll never get out." The UN is still there.

In 1974, following a coup by Greek rightists, Turkish troops invaded and seized a third of the island, establishing a separate Turkish Cypriot government that only Turkey recognizes. The cease-fire line remains in the same place policed by—guess who—UN peacekeepers.

UNFICYP's longstanding mandate has been to "prevent a recurrence of fighting." It has been accused of becoming part of the problem because it freezes an unsustainable status quo! In the divided capital of Nicosia, water comes in one side, and sewage flows out the other. The UN has to mediate that!

Every secretary-general since then has tried to mediate between the two communities. The talks continue.

# The Iran-Iraq War of 1980–88: The Very First Gulf War

The war began when Saddam Hussein took advantage of the overthrow of the Shah to invade Iran. The conflict killed around a million in a trench war that recalled the battles of the First World War. It also saw Iraq slamming hundreds of missiles into Iranian cities and using poison gas against Iranian troops and civilians—and against villages in Iraqi Kurdistan, too.

The Security Council did absolutely nothing until the war burnt itself out and Iraq agreed to a cease-fire. Eventually, in July 1988, Resolution 598 called for a cease-fire and withdrawal to the borders. After a last vindictive spasm of violence, Iraq withdrew its troops by the deadline but sent them to kill some 50,000 Iraqi Kurds instead.

Iran had insisted on a UN commission to determine who started the war. Reporting back after the next Gulf War, the commission laid the blame squarely on Iraq. But this finding was kept quiet because by then the United States was insisting that Iraq pay reparations to Kuwait and its equally wealthy allies, and it did not want any reparations to go to Iran. Iraq ended up paying billions in compensation for decades. Iran did not get a cent.

## Operation Desert Storm, 1991

When Iraq invaded Kuwait in 1990, the UN moved promptly to reverse that action. This was a textbook example of how the UN was supposed to operate. (Usually, it didn't.) But this time, since the Cold War was

over, Russia cooperated with the United States in an action aimed at underlining "the inadmissibility of the acquisition of territory by force."

If Iraqi President Saddam Hussein had held swift elections in Kuwait and withdrawn, he might have had a friendly state on his doorstep. But he didn't. He soon dissolved the puppet government his troops had installed in Kuwait and annexed it as the nineteenth province of Iraq.

The UN immediately imposed sanctions. As had happened in Korea decades earlier, the Security Council franchised the command of the UN operation out to the United States. Even Moscow agreed. So it was the Pentagon that decided when the war was going to start and finish and how it was to be waged. As often, it decided to use massive bombing. In the short, brutal war that drove the Iraqis out of Kuwait, there were huge Iraqi casualties, while the allies' losses were minimal.

Because the sanctions resolutions had no end dates in them, they remained in place for years after most Council members wanted to see them lifted. But the United States, United Kingdom, and France, earlier on, vetoed any attempt to lift them.

## Impunity for Peacekeepers?

Over the years, as the demand for peacekeepers grew, more and more countries provided troops with varying (or inadequate) levels of experience and professionalism. Peacekeepers have been accused of atrocities and sexual violence and exploitation, but the UN has to rely on the countries concerned to discipline their troops, while the organization takes the blame. This is far from being just a developing-world problem: France and Canada have each have had their share of incidents.

In 2016, Ban Ki-moon made history of sorts by apologizing to Haiti for the cholera epidemic that had swept the country after being unwittingly introduced by the poor sanitation of Nepali peacekeepers deployed there in 2010. In the worst traditions of bureaucratic buck-passing, local UN officials had long denied any connection to the peacekeepers, despite plentiful evidence. That denial helped exacerbate the outbreak that ended up affecting three quarters of a million Haitians and killing almost 10,000.

UN officials at HQ had panicked at the prospect of lawsuits in the United States. They denied responsibility, and it took several years of wrangling before Ban Ki-moon admitted the UN's moral responsibility for the outbreak and announced a voluntary fund to mitigate the damage. Some reporters claimed there was pressure from Washington not to admit any liability, since the US administration did not want to go to Congress for more cash.

António Guterres landed his job in the midst of heart-searching about "the blight of sexual exploitation and abuse by some peacekeepers," which, he said, "does irreparable damage to the lives of civilians and to the credibility of the United Nations."

He set modest standards: "At a minimum, they must do no harm. In that spirit, an effective and responsible mission must earn the confidence of the local population." More effectively, he set up a fund to compensate victims and suggested that countries that did not discipline offenders would have UN payments for their troops withheld. He also announced changes to make troop-contributing countries pledge legal action against any peacekeepers who commit crimes.

## Somalia

Unusually for an African country, Somalia's people share the same language and religion and live in contiguous territory. But they are divided into clans, and during the Cold War these became increasingly heavily armed since the government switched its allegiance between the two superpowers several times, and each time it did so its new patrons poured huge new arsenals into the country. (Somalia is also located in a spot on the coast of the Red Sea that many people once described as "strategic.")

## Success Story!

One of the most effective peacekeeping forces was stationed on the Macedonian border with Serbia and Kosovo in 1995. UNPREDEP was the first purely preemptive peacekeeping deployment. There was no actual conflict, but since Belgrade had engineered astrife on all its other borders the Council assumed the worst.

Unusually, it had a large US contingent, which was an effective warning to Serbian president Slobodan Milosevic to back off. UNPREDEP's deployment ensured one of the few peaceful boundaries in the former Yugoslavia, until its mandate renewal was vetoed by China because Macedonia had opened diplomatic relations with Taiwan.

That made Beijing look petty, but by then NATO had forces in the Balkans, so Milosevic was deterred from launching any military action against Macedonia anyway. But when China tried to veto UN action in Haiti, which had also recognized Taiwan, Latin American and Caribbean diplomats had quiet words with their Chinese counterparts about the regional consequences for China's reputation, and Beijing backed down.

By 1991, civil war, exacerbated by famine, had resulted in the disappearance of the old government. Clan militias, armed to the teeth, roamed the cities, sometimes robbing relief convoys while thousands starved. Everyone agreed the UN should step in.

In December 1992, US Marines stormed ashore in full invasion mode, to be greeted by the media and their cameras that were lined up to record their arrival. The Marines' presence confused the issue. Some of the US forces were under UN control and some were not. Washington refused to do what Boutros-Ghali wanted, which was to disarm the militias, so there were perennial problems deciding who was really in charge.

Scores of peacekeepers were killed and wounded in ambushes and firefights, notably in the "Black Hawk Down" incident. A UN report suggested that some of these clashes resulted from UN or US attempts to take on one militia in preference to another.

In 1994, the United States pulled out, leaving the militias still armed to the teeth, and with the one warlord that the Marines had specially targeted freer and stronger than ever before. Somalia remains very unstable today. But the events there had a lasting effect on world affairs since the "Black Hawk Down" incident stampeded President Clinton into issuing Presidential Decisions Directive 25 (PDD 25), which banned any US support for UN peacekeeping operations "unless vital American interests were involved."

In the early stages, that seemed to mean that the US delegates would not authorize any peacekeeping operations that did not directly serve US policy. Soon enough, hundreds of thousands of Rwandans found out that it was not "a US interest" to save them from massacre when the United States prevented the UN from sending reinforcements to bolster the tiny, embattled UN force in Rwanda.

These operations took place "BC," Before the Courts. Later operations such as Rwanda and in the Balkans and in Sierra Leone gave birth to a new era. With the establishment of international courts and tribunals, perpetrators no longer had complete impunity and stood some, albeit faint, chance of punishment for their misdeeds.

# Do what we do, not what we say!

Governments don't always want the UN to succeed. They often just want to pass the buck. Some leaders appease their own public opinion and defer to legality by referring issues to the UN—and then make sure it can't do the job. One US Ambassador to the UN, Daniel Patrick Moynihan (later a senator from New York), wrote this in his memoirs about the time after the Security Council had condemned Indonesia's seizure of East Timor and Morocco's of Western Sahara in the mid-1970s:

> China altogether backed Fretilin [the Timorese Liberation movement] in Timor, and lost. In Spanish Sahara, Russia completely backed Algeria, and its front [in Western Sahara], known as Polisario, and lost. In both instances the United States wished things to turn out as they did, and worked to bring this about. The Department of State desired that the United Nations prove utterly ineffective in whatever measures it undertook. The task was given to me, and I carried it forward with no inconsiderable success.

One-third of the population of East Timor died when Indonesia defied UN resolutions calling on it to leave the country. Later, political changes in Indonesia itself led to Indonesia withdrawing from East Timor, though Indonesian-backed militias continued to commit massive violence there. Many members of the UN mission there refused to obey UN orders to leave the country. They stayed behind to try to protect the victims until the UN authorized a robust peacekeeping force from Australia. East

Timor is now independent, and a UN member as Timor Leste.

By contrast, Morocco, also a US ally, just stayed put in Western Sahara, whose people are mostly still surviving in refugee camps in the desert fifty years later. Morocco still refuses to honor Security Council resolutions and will not allow a referendum on self-determination in Western Sahara, despite the presence of a peacekeeping

mission, MINURSO, whose official name is United Nations Mission for the *Referendum* in Western Sahara!

The UN and its members often will not act to reverse occupations. Nonetheless, despite Moynihan, "the inadmissibility of acquiring territory by force" is still a core UN principle.

Thus, though Morocco has many allies, no other country recognizes its claim to Western Sahara. Similarly, no other country recognizes Israel's claims to occupied East Jerusalem or the Golan Heights—and even its claim to West Jerusalem is not recognized, since the UN's 1947 Partition Plan for Palestine ruled that the whole of Jerusalem should be a separate, internationally-administered entity.

The US Congress has passed many resolutions instructing the administration to move the US Embassy in Israel to Jerusalem. But the State Department has always managed, at least until the Trump era, to keep within international law and resist the urgings of Congress.

More recently, although Russia took Crimea, we can confidently predict that its control there will not be internationally recognized until either Ukraine or the UN agrees. Aggression and conquest were what started World War II, so opposition to them lies at the heart of the UN Charter.

As for Senator Moynihan, he died a revered elder statesman.

# ■ BOMBS AWAY! THE UN FOR DISARMERS!

## Ending the Scourge of War: Getting Rid of Whole Classes of Weapons

There is a lengthy history of attempts to keep war "civilized." From 1899, international conventions outlawed dum-dum bullets (designed to break apart in the body) and, later, chemical and gas weapons.

Apart from the use of gas during World War I and the Iran-Iraq War, and more recently in Syria, belligerents have been more restrained in the use of chemical and biological weapons than we might have expected. It was almost certainly more from fear of retaliation than from morals. (Of course, major nations have also kept large stocks of chemical weapons, along with some ability to put together biological weapons at fairly short notice.)

In 1972, the Convention on the Prohibition of the Development, Production and Stockpiling of Bacteriological and Toxin Weapons and on their Destruction (BTWC) was the first multilateral treaty

categorically banning a class of weapon, but they could not set up a monitoring organization to check compliance. The title does not actually prohibit using biological weapons, but later conferences stressed that using them was indeed illegal.

There was more success with chemical weapons, and the convention against them set up the Organization for the Prohibition of Chemical Weapons (OPCW), in The Hague, which has a "special relationship" with the UN and the ICJ but also a lot of autonomy.

In 2016, the OPCW found that such weapons had been used in Syria, but it was not able to identify the perpetrators.

## Landmines

With advances in technology, land mines and antipersonnel weapons are deadly killers that haunt former battlefields for decades, slaughtering up to 20,000 people a year, mostly civilians in former conflict zones. In 1997, backed by Canada, the International Campaign to Ban Land-mines forced the Ottawa Convention "on the Prohibition of the Use, Stockpiling, Production, and Transfer of Anti-Personnel Mines

and on their Destruction." The campaign and its leader, Jody Williams, won the Nobel Peace Prize.

By 2015, more than 160 countries had signed. China, Russia, and the United States did not sign it, though Washington declared acceptance of its terms, except in Korea, where the US-dominated UN command still lays mines in the Demilitarized Zone between the north and south—as does the North Korean military.

The UN's Mine Action Service (part of the Department of Peacekeeping Operations) has helped lift and destroy more than 46 million mines around the world.

In 2008, the Convention on Cluster Munitions came into force. Its member states vow to abstain from owning or using cluster weapons. By 2015, it had 116 signatories.

## Bombs, including Nuclear Bombs

The 1932 Geneva Convention banned bombing civilians. It was not a very effective ban, and the Nazis at Guernica, the Italians in Ethiopia, and the Japanese in China soon showed international prohibition of bombing was going to be as unsuccessful as the US prohibition of alcohol.

In World War II, both sides bombed cities. Then, and in conflicts afterward, thousands of civilians died even when militaries and their air forces claimed they were aiming their bombs at military targets. But while thousand-bomber air fleets or powerful land- or sea-based artillery could destroy a city, nuclear weapons threaten to destroy the world.

The General Assembly first met just a few months after the United States dropped nuclear bombs over Hiroshima and Nagasaki. It suggested setting up an Atomic Energy Commission to control the holding, development, and use of nuclear weapons—with no veto. The Soviets saw this as a means of preserving the US advantage, so the proposal stalled.

In 1953, US President Eisenhower proposed an international "Atoms for Peace" Program. The Soviets, whose nuclear arsenal was

EVOLUTION....

not as big as his, once again objected. Then in 1954, the International Atomic Energy Authority (IAEA) was finally set up. Some saw it as a means of selling nuclear power to the world.

Like many organizations suggested by the United States, the IAEA was established "under the aegis" of the UN, with "a special relationship with the General Assembly," though the two parties still kept their distance from each other. The IAEA's first director was a Republican congressman, Sterling Cole, whose appointment was met with resentment from many assembly delegates.

In 1963, popular uproar at the amount of fallout from bomb testing led to the Nuclear Test Ban Treaty, which stopped surface tests. That was followed in 1968 by the conclusion of the Nuclear Non-Proliferation Treaty (NPT). It banned any *additional* nations from acquiring nuclear weapons and relied on the IAEA to monitor compliance. At that stage, four members of the P5 already had nuclear weapons. In 1971, when Beijing took over the "China" seat at the UN (and its P5 seat in the Security Council), all five of them had nuclear weapons.

Israel never signed the NPT and so could refuse IAEA inspections. India's continuing development of nuclear weapons, along with Israeli nukes, fueled Pakistan's attempts to develop an "Islamic bomb."

People and governments that claimed that the NPT gave undue privileges to the P5 had a point. The existing, "recognized" nuclear-weapons states had promised to disarm as well—but it soon became clear that they were only kidding.

The last white Prime Minister of South Africa, F.W. De Klerk, was an unlikely hero of disarmament, but in 1993, he announced that his government was giving up the nuclear weapons that no one (except Israel) knew for certain that he had. He was no pacifist. He just did not want Nelson Mandela and South Africa's new majority government to have the bomb.

In 1994, North Korea announced that it was withdrawing from the NPT, and over the years that followed it slowly advanced to possession of a small, fairly primitive nuclear arsenal. Thus today, there are a total of nine nuclear-armed nations. This might look bad, but if it were not for the UN and the associated treaties, there could have been dozens of nuclear powers in place by now.

Equally good for health and non-proliferation has been the Comprehensive Test Ban Treaty, which does not have a UN organization to implement it. The organization is to be set up 180 days after the Treaty has been ratified by the 44 countries listed with nuclear

technology. India, North Korea, and Pakistan have neither signed nor ratified the treaty, while China, Egypt, Iran, Israel, and the United States have signed but not ratified it.

Despite that, public upset over testing and fallout has had some effect, and apart from the (very) special case of North Korea, which tests underground, there have been no nuclear tests since Pakistan's last blast in 1998.

# SECTION 4

# The UN and Human Rights

## ■ HUMAN RIGHTS VS. NATIONAL SOVEREIGNTY

The Charter said the UN should "reaffirm faith in fundamental human rights." Article 55 called for universal respect for, and observance of, human rights and fundamental freedoms for all without distinction as to race, sex, language, or religion. But when governments get together, the Charter's emphasis on state sovereignty often trump such mentions of human rights.

In February 2017, Zeid Ra'ad al-Hussein, the UN's High Commissioner for Human Rights (and the UN official formerly known as Prince) said:

> Human rights was placed in the preamble of the UN Charter not as the last or a third pillar or as some literary flourish. It was there, it came first, human rights were viewed as the necessary starting condition, because on 26 June 1945, the day of the Charter's signing, killing on a scale hitherto unknown to humans had only just come to an end, with cities across the world pulverized and still smoking, monuments to immense human malevolence and stupidity.

The delegations understood that only by first accepting fundamental human rights could all else—durable peace, and success in development—become possible.

ECOSOC set up the Commission on Human Rights to draw up the Universal Declaration of Human Rights. While Eleanor Roosevelt provided much of the dynamism behind it, the declaration was drafted first by a Canadian, John Peters Humphrey, and then by the French delegate, René Cassin. The drafting commission also included Chinese diplomat Peng Chun Chang and Lebanese delegate Charles Malik, who imparted an Arab angle to the document but in later life became the leader of the Lebanese Front, whose main aim was to preserve Christian rule in the majority Muslim country.

From the UN itself, African-American diplomat Ralph Bunche played an active part in composing the declaration, while the committee that finalized the draft included Hansa Mehta, an Indian woman whom the British had earlier imprisoned for fighting for independence. She took its phrase "All **men** are born free and equal and substituted "all **human beings** are born free and equal." Other members of the commission included Hernan Santa Cruz, a childhood friend of Chile's later-martyred President Salvador Allende, and Charles Dukes, ex-President of the British Trade Union Congress.

That so many countries still fear the resonance of the declaration's ringing language shows its effectiveness. According to the Guinness Book of Records, it is the most translated document in the world, in 440 different languages, so people everywhere can and do quote it! Indeed, its power went extra-terrestrial: there is even a Klingon version.

> The rights set out in [the Universal Declaration of Human Rights] identify many of the root causes of conflict, but equally they provide real world solutions through real change on the ground.
> **António Guterres, 2017**

The General Assembly's adoption of the Universal Declaration on December 10, 1948, with no dissent, gives the lie to people who claim it tries to impose "Western" values. (As Ralph Bunche could testify, one form of "Western values" meant that across whole swathes of the old Confederacy only whites could vote. Those were definitely not the values he sought.)

In the lead-up to the Universal Declaration's fiftieth anniversary in 1998, concerned delegations and organizations met at the UN to consider how best to commemorate it. They agreed that by that time any attempt to revise the text would result in a much weaker document.

Under pressure from some governments and the NGOs, in 2006 the Assembly set up the Human Rights Council. Its forty-seven members are elected by a majority of the whole General Assembly. The aim of that was to avoid having recidivist human rights offenders getting on the council and thwarting investigations into each other, though that goal was certainly not always met.

On the Human Rights Council there have been messy compromises, mainly to allay the suspicions voiced by diplomats from many developing countries who had noticed that most prosecutions of war criminals were against their leaders, while the leaders of richer countries who launched wars and committed atrocities seemed always to escape punishment.

The formation of the Human Rights Council did mark some improvement. But in 2015, the council did include the representatives of China, Cuba, Kazakhstan, Russia, and Saudi Arabia, countries whose repressive human rights records and limited democracy were under scrutiny by the council's rapporteurs—along with the United States and the United Kingdom, who still had not atoned in any way for their illegal invasion of Iraq and the atrocities that followed that invasion.

In 1993, the UN had established a separate, senior position called the UN High Commissioner for Human Rights, with some powers of investigation. The secretary-general appoints the high commissioner, but most appointees have been public figures in their own right, such as South Africa's Navi Pillay, the former Irish President Mary Robinson, or Zeid Ra'ad al-Hussein of Jordan.

It is worth remembering, though, that Robinson was finally forced to quit because of pressure from hardline pro-Israeli American politicians because she condemned Israeli behavior in the Occupied Territories. Later, when President

*Former President of Ireland Mary Robinson became High Commissioner for Human Rights.*

Obama awarded her the Presidential Medal of Freedom, forty-five Republican legislators complained of her allegedly failed, biased record as Commissioner. (Most of the rest of the world took that as a strong endorsement of her achievements in office.)

> The whole human rights structure is based on the accountability of governments.
> **Mary Robinson**

The Commissioner and the Council's best weapon is their ability to "name and shame" delinquent countries. The desperate lengths to which such countries will go as they try to deflect or evade such criticism suggest that it actually works, up to a point!

## The Special International Criminal Tribunals, 1992–2002

Starting in 1992, the international community found it could deploy more than shame. Increasingly, wrong-doers who once could have claimed sovereign immunity have been indicted and tried. Generals and politicians now have to check with their lawyers as well as their travel agents before going abroad. In part, this is because some countries such as Spain have adopted "universal jurisdiction" so they can try cases no matter where the crime was committed. In part, it is because many

governments and the UN have strengthened the mechanisms of inter-national criminal justice.

As we have seen, the International Court of Justice adjudicates only disputes between nations. By contrast, the International Criminal Court, the ICC, and the interim criminal tribunals that preceded it were designed to try and punish *individuals* who have committed atrocities, in circumstances in which national courts either can't or won't prosecute them.

In the 1990s, the wars in the "Former Yugoslavia" and Rwanda involved horrors of a kind not seen in Europe since 1945. Around the world, many people worried that the perpetrators would get away unpunished. In 1992, the Security Council set up a Commission of Experts to investigate the suspected large-scale crimes being commit-ted in the former Yugoslavia. Some cynics thought that was just a ploy to take pressure off governments to intervene, but the investigations were so devastating and detailed that the Security Council was forced to go after the perpetrators.

The Commission of Experts' report jump-started the establishment of the International Criminal Tribunal for Former Yugoslavia (ICTY), which was headquartered in The Hague, Netherlands. ICTY had its own prosecutors and even its own prison cells, which it leased from the Dutch and other governments. By 2015, it had indicted 161 people.

In 1994, in the wake of the ethnic massacres in Rwanda, the Security Council set up a similar court to try the atrocities there—ICTR, head-quartered in Arusha, Tanzania. When this court approached its wind-down in 2015, it had indicted ninety-three alleged perpetrators.

The UN was also involved in a hybrid international/Cambodian court, the "Extraordinary Chambers in the Courts of Cambodia." This court has been much less successful than ICTY or ICTR, since the Cambodian government wanted to protect its own former comrades in the Khmer Rouge who were charged with mass murder. This venture has cost $300 million to try five accused so far—and two of them died before they were sentenced.

There was also a proposal to establish a similar court for Timor Leste. But the commission investigating how to deal with the atrocities committed there decided to offer amnesty to alleged perpetrators in the interests of peace and reconciliation. Ban Ki-moon then boycotted the commission. On principle, he explained, the UN did not approve of granting amnesty for human rights violations.

More successful was the UN-convened Special Court for Sierra Leone, which successfully tried and punished murderous leaders for their actions during the civil war there.

## The International Criminal Court (ICC)

The special tribunals have now almost all wound down, because in 2002, 160 nations, acting together, established the International Criminal Court, a permanent body that, like so many other international bodies, is based in the Dutch seat of government, The Hague.

The rules for the ICC had been defined in the 1998 Rome Treaty. They had to allow for the tastes of different legal traditions and many suspicious countries. The Treaty's main principle was that the ICC prosecutor could bring charges only in very closely defined circumstances and only when it had been established that the relevant national courts were unable or unwilling to do so.

The Court's mandate includes genocide, war crimes, and crimes against humanity. Its power is not retrospective, so it covers only crimes committed after July 1, 2002. It can go after those directly responsible, as well as others who may be liable for the crimes, for example, by aiding, abetting, or otherwise assisting. Especially important is the doctrine of "command responsibility," namely that those who order crimes are as guilty as those who actually commit them.

A state or the Security Council can refer cases to the prosecutor, or the prosecutor can start investigations on her or his own account, but the accused has to be a national of a state that is a party to the Rome Treaty, or the crime must be committed on the territory of such a state.

The US delegation in the Rome negotiations supported the basic principles of this court, but, faced with isolationist pressures at home, the Clinton administration negotiated lots of exemptions to reduce the risk of any Americans being prosecuted. President Clinton signed the

treaty on his last day in office, but the Senate was never willing to ratify it, and after George W. Bush became president in 2001 he appointed John Bolton, a consistent UN-hater, to lead the opposition to it. Bush authorized Bolton to "unsign" the treaty.

Bolton also obsessively bullied dozens of small countries into signing bilateral agreements promising never to hand over US citizens to the ICC. In 2002, the United States threatened to veto the renewal of all UN peacekeeping unless its troops were granted immunity from ICC prosecution. As a compromise, that year the Security Council passed Resolution 1422, which allows immunity to peacekeepers coming from countries that are not in the ICC. The resolution was supposed to be renewable annually, and the Council did renew it once, in 2003. But later that year and in early 2004, the pictures of US troops abusing Iraqi prisoners at Abu Ghraib prison persuaded the Council not to renew the exemption again, and Washington was too embarrassed to press the issue.

Paradoxically, the United States, which has "unsigned" the Rome Treaty, now joins in calls to the Security Council to apply it to other countries, with the tacit support of Russia and China. (Neither of them have ratified it either!)

One nightmare for the US and Israel happened when Palestine was accepted as a "State Party" to the Rome Treaty and signed it in 2015. So Israeli (and Palestinian) behavior, on the territory of Palestine—such as during the invasions of Gaza—could be liable to ICC prosecution.

## Truth and Reconciliation: An Alternative

The "Truth and Reconciliation" process pioneered by South African leaders such as Desmond Tutu and Nelson Mandela was based on the idea that building future peace and stability was more important than engaging in backward-looking retribution. It also implicitly accepted that both sides had transgressed in some measure during the many centuries of conflict in South Africa between the white settlers and the area's indigenous peoples.

Whether confession is good for the soul or not, those national liberation leaders saw free admission and repentance as a better guarantee against future violence than endless prosecutions. South Africa's Truth and Reconciliation Commission (TRC) did reveal many details of how Apartheid had functioned, often in return for amnesty, but many victims saw it as a whitewash for the perpetrators.

# ■ THE EMERGENCE OF R2P, THE RESPONSIBILITY TO PROTECT

It was all very well to set up courts to try mass murderers, but this raised an important question: If international organizations could punish murder, why couldn't they *prevent* atrocities from happening in the first place?

Under cover of "national sovereignty," governments have killed and abused their own citizens for centuries. But increasingly in recent decades live television has shown the murders while they happen, or their aftermath when satellites reveal the mass graves and the killing fields. In the aftermath of the Cold War, as Secretary-General Pérez De Cuéllar concluded, the world "was clearly witnessing what is probably an irresistible shift in public attitudes toward the belief that the defense of the oppressed in the name of morality should prevail over frontiers and legal documents."

There were precedents for joint action that ignored national boundaries. Two centuries earlier, governments had agreed to suppress the slave trade on the open seas, and pirates were deemed enemies of all mankind. Indeed, one of the earliest UN decisions was to adopt the Genocide Convention in 1948, which actually mandates states to intervene to prevent genocide—though none ever has.

Another breach of the sovereignty dogma was the isolation of Apartheid South Africa. As early as 1946, India had complained about the white South African government's discrimination against Indians living there, which violated treaties and the Charter's reference to human rights. Pretoria responded that this was a domestic issue.

At that point the UN had few African members. But in 1952, four years after South Africa officially introduced its policy of Apartheid, India and twelve other Asian states raised an official complaint against the policy with the Security Council. The word *apartheid* means "apart-hood" or "segregation," but as in the southern United States, it really meant white domination. In 1973, the UN finally officially declared that Apartheid as formally practiced in South Africa was a crime. Like the Genocide Convention, the Apartheid Convention chipped away at the idea that the dogma of state sovereignty gave governments the absolute right to do whatever they wanted at home.

In 1974, the General Assembly barred the South African delegation from participating, and three years later, while Jimmy Carter was US President, the Security Council mandated an arms embargo against South Africa. (With tacit US backing, Israel continued to arm the Apartheid regime. It even helped it to develop nuclear weapons.)

It took many more years of UN resolutions before South Africa finally held democratic elections in 1994. That ended Apartheid forever, and the South African delegation was able to return to the General Assembly.

## Cambodia and the UN

After his country gained independence from France, Prince Norodom Sihanouk of Cambodia maneuvered successfully for years to keep his country neutral in the wars in Indochina, even though the Vietnamese used the border country to supply the war effort in South Vietnam. However, the US launched devastatingly destructive bombings against the country from 1969 to 1973 and inspired a coup against the Sihanouk government. The unpopular US-installed government fell in turn to the communist Khmer Rouge in 1975. They proceeded to mass murder their "class enemies" and political opponents, empty the cities, and declare the "Year Zero." Estimates for the number of Cambodians killed or dead of starvation and disease range from 1.7 to 2.5 million people. In response to increasing Khmer Rouge border raids, Vietnam invaded Cambodia in 1979, installing a friendly government of Khmer Rouge defectors including Hun Sen, who became prime minister in 1985.

With support from China, the United States, and the United Kingdom, the defeated Khmer Rouge held the country's UN seat as Democratic Kampuchea until 1990, even though they only had effective control of a small strip of land on the Thai border far from the capital. Secretary-General Perez De Cuéllar convened multilateral peace talks—it was clearly an international problem since so many hostile powers had created it! There was increasing pressure from NGOs and others disturbed and guilty that such a massive, genocidal tragedy had happened with no serious international resistance, and indeed much collusion. There was, if not guilt, enough embarrassment to go around.

By the time the parties agreed to peace talks they had fought to a stalemate on the ground and their foreign sponsors were giving up on them. The Soviets were making up with China, so Moscow pulled back from supporting Vietnam and China, and the West and Thailand had lost interest in supporting the Khmer Rouge. With the exception of Sihanouk as figurehead, none of the parties were acceptable to the others. As so often happens, since the country was broken in pieces, the UN was mandated to put the country back together again, and Australia, which had temporary ambitions to be an Asian power, managed to nudge the P5 into going along. There was a precedent with Namibia, a conflict also orphaned by the end of the Cold War, although at least Namibia had a functioning economy and government, albeit white dominated, that the UN could work with.

Between the changes of government and the war, the Khmer Rouge policy of emptying the cities, and eliminating all previous administrative structures, the UN had to rebuild the country from scratch. In 1992, the UN sent in the UN Transitional Authority in Cambodia

(UNTAC) to run the still war-traumatized country. UNTAC was the biggest peacekeeping mission ever at that point and the first to take over the entire administration of a country, organizing and running elections for a new government. They were supposed to disarm the various factions but had mixed success, and the peacekeepers were of mixed quality, with few of them prepared to stand up to the armed factions. The large Japanese contingent, when confronted by the Khmer Rouge, seemed to prove how well the country had adopted its pacifist constitution!

In 1993, the UN pulled out and declared success, but in reality, it was a heavily qualified success. There *were* elections, but even though Hun Sen lost them, he managed to become Prime Minster anyway. He is still there, while opposition leaders went into exile. And as we have seen, UN assistance to the Cambodian courts has been expensive but ineffective in trying former leaders. None of the great powers who were so eager to cause Cambodia's problems to begin with has had any enthusiasm for reopening the issues.

## The Machismo Factor

The atrocities in Cambodia, along with horrendous government-organized mass killings in East Pakistan (later Bangladesh) and Uganda in the 1970s, added to a growing feeling that the world should do something about such crimes. But when neighbors did move in, it was officially a defensive response to attacks, not humanitarian intervention.

Humanitarian intervention was invoked in the case of Iraq in 1991 when, in the closing days of Operation Desert Storm in 1991, President George H. W. Bush openly called upon the Kurds in the north and the Shia and the Marsh Arabs in the south to rise up against Baghdad. But then, when they did, he and his military commanders decided not to intervene to help them, since the UN's mandate had been only to liberate Kuwait, not to force "regime change" in Iraq.

The first President Bush, who had previously been the US Ambassador to the UN, actually respected international law in an old-fashioned way! He presumably simply *hoped* that Saddam Hussein's

regime would collapse. So, the US stood by and watched as Saddam Hussein's air force and army visited bloody revenge on the rebels.

Several prominent international figures, including former British Prime Minister Margaret Thatcher and Danielle Mitterrand, the wife of the French president, called loudly for protection for the Iraqi Kurds in particular. Many Western commentators questioned what the whole Gulf War had been about if this could still happen. The French government started talking about launching a military action with humanitarian goals (a "humanitarian intervention") in Iraq. But in the UN the lawyers worried. After all, Hitler had used exactly that excuse to "rescue" Sudeten Germans from Czechoslovakia and thus invade Czechoslovakia!

Anyway, there was no majority in the Security Council for action. Britain, France, and the United States declared (and for the next twelve years enforced) a "No Fly Zone" over much of Iraq and claimed that it had a UN mandate—though SG Pérez De Cuéllar was at pains to deny that this was so.

# The Balkanization of the UN

Old doctrines of sovereignty continued to confront the public's idea that the world had a duty to victims of inhumane behavior. When the Yugoslav Federation split apart in 1992, most of its parts were recognized as independent states and admitted to UN membership, which should have guaranteed them Kuwait-style anti-annexation insurance. But they had no oil, which reduced Washington's interest. As US Secretary of State James Baker said at one point, "We don't have a dog in this fight."

As tensions built inside the splintering Yugoslavia, the Security Council passed a resolution proposed by the Serbs, who controlled the Yugoslav UN seat, to embargo all arms shipments to the territory. They had their own huge stockpiles of weaponry, so the embargo was tantamount to disarming the victims.

When the Bosnian government asked for monitors along their frontier with Serbia, the Council refused because then there was no precedent for "preemptive" peacekeeping. The Serb military soon

103

invaded Bosnia and started besieging the capital, Sarajevo, and other major cities.

Even the countries that had recognized the new Balkan states would not send soldiers to help them, though they did impose sanctions on Serbia. In the end, governments reluctantly agreed to provide a small UN peacekeeping force whose mandate was originally restricted to safeguarding humanitarian convoys. To save face, the Council also authorized an investigation into the reports of major rights violations in Bosnia and other formerly Yugoslav countries. That investigation ended up embarrassing them deeply by documenting widespread atrocities there.

In 1993, the International Court of Justice ruled that actual genocide was taking place as thousands of Bosnians had been killed or deported during what the Serbs called "ethnic cleansing." The Genocide Convention made it a duty for signatories to intervene to end the genocide. None of them did.

In Bosnia, the United Nations Protection Force (UNPROFOR), kept people fed, while taking neutrality to its limits. It watched and counted the Serbs firing on the city, counted how many artillery shells and mortar rounds were fired, and even enforced the siege of Sarajevo, refusing to allow civilians to leave the city.

What turned the tide was the fall of the so-called UN "safe haven" of Srebrenica in 1995. There, the Serbian forces carried out what Kofi Annan called "the worst crime on European soil since the Second World War" and what the International Criminal Tribunal on the former Yugoslavia called "acts of genocide." It was the UN's worst hour. The Dutch contingent of the UN force in Srebrenica chased out civilians who tried to seek shelter in the UN compound and handed over their own weapons and vehicles to the Serbian attackers, who went on to massacre thousands of Bosnian boys and men.

Kofi Annan later said that "the tragedy of Srebrenica will forever haunt the history of the United Nations." For once, it also haunted the perpetrators. General Ratko Mladic, Bosnian Serb leader Radovan Karadzic, and Serbian president Slobodan Milosevic were all eventually brought before the International Tribunal for the former Yugoslavia.

## UN Hero! Romeo Dallaire: Blame and Shame to Go Around

The small central African country of Rwanda was one of several pre–World War II issues that came back to haunt the UN a lot later. For several decades after it became independent from Belgium in 1962, there was low-level civil war in the country, sometimes purely political and sometimes pitting members of the country's Tutsi minority against its Hutu majority. In 1993, the warring parties reached a tentative peace agreement, and the UN sent a small peacekeeping force called UNAMIR to oversee its implementation.

In 1994, Major-General Romeo Dallaire, the Canadian commander of UNAMIR, discovered plans that some Hutu extremists had for a massacre of Tutsis and moderate Hutus. The plans even described where the weapons the plotters had amassed were stockpiled. He told UN Headquarters about the plans. They ordered him not to try to seize the weapons, but to report the plot to the Rwandan government—whose members were among those planning the mass murder!

Abandoned by the world, Dallaire and his peacekeepers managed to save 30,000 designated victims. But between 800,000 and a million others were sacrificed on the altar of national sovereignty because (at President Clinton's urging) the Security Council refused to send any reinforcements for UNAMIR. Dallaire returned to Canada traumatized, but he became an advocate for timely international intervention.

"In their greatest hour of need, the world failed the people of Rwanda. . . . At that time of evil . . . the international community and the United Nations could not muster the political will to confront it," Kofi Annan commented later.

To complicate matters, the French, who had long backed the genocidal Rwandan government, secured a mandate from the Security Council to send in their own alleged "peacekeeping" force, Operation

Turquoise. Other council members were deeply suspicious of the French but were unwilling to send any of their own troops. The French force defended the fleeing government supporters from the victorious rebels and let them panic millions of Hutus into fleeing to Congo and other neighboring countries where thousands of them died of cholera and starvation.

Soon thereafter, militias linked to the new, post-genocide govern-ment in Rwanda also deployed to Congo, saying they wanted to pre-vent the genocidists from regrouping there. But the arrival of the rival Rwandan militias into the Congo brought about one of the longest and bloodiest wars in modern Africa, which has continued there since 1994 and has involved the deployment of massive numbers of peacekeepers.

If President Clinton had responded positively to General Dallaire's early appeals for help, the US share of the peacekeeping bill for Rwanda would have been $36 million. As it was, Washington spent $500 mil-lion on humanitarian relief after the genocide, and untold sums on humanitarian relief since then, in Congo. The ethics and the finances were equally flawed.

To the relief of many, however, many of the leaders of the genocide were tried and imprisoned by the International Tribunal for Rwanda.

## Kosovo

Kosovo was an autonomous province of Serbia with an ethnic Albanian majority, but in 1987, Serbian President Slobodan Milosevic dissolved their government and replaced it with a form of apartheid, so the Serbian minority ran the place. Years of passive Gandhian resistance had gotten the Kosovars nowhere, and some began armed resistance, which Belgrade met with massive repression despite cautions from the Security Council. The UN had Srebrenica haunting its memory. In 1998/99, Milosevic's troops drove many, if not most, of the Kosovars over the borders, while the Russian veto stopped Security Council action.

Milosevic was pushing against the boundaries of the Charter's Chapter VII. By deporting refugees across the border, he had trans-formed domestic mayhem into a threat to international peace and security, risking all-out war in the Balkans. But the Russians would not accept that—and they had a veto!

In 1999, NATO unilaterally began bombing Serbia over the Kosovo issue. But President Clinton said at the beginning that there was no question of using ground troops. The bombing had little military

*Kosovar refugees flee from Serbian forces.*

effect and eroded support for attacks. When Russia tried to oppose the bombing at the UN, it could not get a majority, and the United States and United Kingdom did not try to get UN endorsement for the bombing because of the Russian veto. So it was a stalemate at the Security Council.

In the end, NATO decided on a ground invasion—and Milosevic immediately surrendered! The Security Council in Resolution 1244 agreed to a temporary settlement, with the deployment of a new peacekeeping force called KFOR that would have both NATO and Russian troops, along with a civilian UN Mission that ran the province (badly), almost as a UN trusteeship.

Kosovo is now independent, but Russia still blocks its application for UN membership. Legally flawed, the operation still did achieve the return of all the Kosovar refugees. The whole episode fed into the growing international debate on intervention and state sovereignty.

# R2P: The Responsibility to Protect

Many people wondered whether the concept of "humanitarian intervention" had any legs at all. After all, governments set up the UN because of violations of national sovereignty and aggression by the Axis powers. Maybe they were only kidding about the "We, the peoples" bit. But the US did not want the UN ending segregation in the South any more than the Soviets wanted it to close down the Gulag.

The Charter says sternly, "Nothing contained in the present Charter shall authorize the United Nations to intervene in matters which are essentially within the domestic jurisdiction of any state or shall require the Members to submit such matters to settlement under the present Charter; but this principle shall not prejudice the application of enforcement measures under Chapter VII."

The Charter is very hard to change because of the veto! So, in response to Kosovo, Rwanda, and Srebrenica, Kofi Annan quietly rewrote international law at the 60th Anniversary World Summit General Assembly of the UN, in 2005. His Summit Declaration reinterpreted the Charter by deciding that *internal* mayhem could threaten international peace and security—and thus trigger Security Council

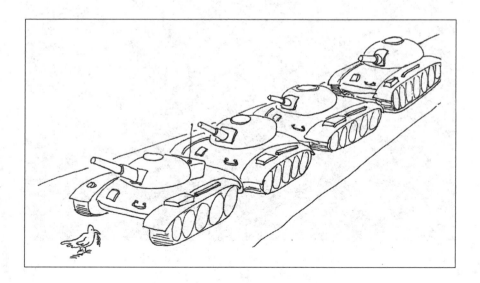

action, including Chapter VII. He persuaded all the government heads to endorse the Responsibility to Protect (R2P) in the case of "national authorities manifestly failing to protect their populations from genocide, war crimes, ethnic cleansing, and crimes against humanity."

No country voted against this effective overturning of the UN Charter's dogma of absolute sovereignty. But international law grows slowly, so many jurists have been surprised at how quickly the R2P concept took off. It was even used by Russia, for example, to justify its interventions in neighboring countries, although Moscow vetoed attempts to apply its principles elsewhere.

## Arab Spring

R2P's debut really came in the Middle East. In 2011, during the so-called Arab Spring, Ban Ki-moon showed how far the doctrine of state sovereignty had eroded when he broke with UN precedent by calling

*Libya's Muammar Qaddafi in his last performance at UNGA.*

for President Hosni Mubarak of Egypt to step down after the repression of protests in Cairo. Ban also condemned Bahrain's brutal crackdown on demonstrators. This all caused a brief outrage among Arab diplomats, but they forgot about it when Mubarak left office a week later. Most of them also overcame their qualms about the intervention of outside powers when the Arab League supported armed intervention against Muammar Qaddafi in Libya.

With the League's support, the Security Council passed Resolution 1973 in the face of Qaddafi's killings and threats against rebellious Libyans. It barely passed by ten votes. Russia, China, Brazil, Germany, and India all abstained—but no one cast a veto it.

Resolution 1973 called for action to end the "systematic violation of human rights, including arbitrary detentions, enforced disappearances, torture, and summary executions." It authorized countries "acting in cooperation with the Secretary-General, to take all necessary measures . . . to protect civilians and civilian populated areas under threat of attack in the Libyan Arab Jamahiriya, including Benghazi, while excluding a foreign occupation force of any form on any part of Libyan territory."

The drafters were looking back at the shameless abuse of the Iraq War resolutions by Britain and the United States two decades before, so the resolution had many layers of international monitoring and control and there were so many parties involved that it was impossible to control.

One strange assumption is that "regime change" is out of bounds, which begs the question of how to stop a genocidal regime *without* overthrowing it! After all, the UN owes its very existence to forcible regime change in Berlin and Tokyo! However, the UN is an association of governments, and their big "no-no" tends to be . . . the overthrow of governments.

The resolution's exclusion of a "foreign occupation force" meant that the battles on the ground in Libya were fought by locals—and they had their own big grudges, as they showed with their torturing and lynching of Qaddafi. Bomber aircraft are not, anyway, very effective at peacekeeping, let alone nation-building, so NATO's planes became the rebels' de-facto air force with little pretense of impartiality.

The outcome, apart from misery for the Libyans, was to confirm the worst fears that the Russians and others had that the NATO countries and friends would stretch any UN resolution that sought humanitarian goals into one that led to forcible regime change. The West's actions in Libya then formed an essential backdrop to the way the Russians (and Chinese) viewed the West's intentions in Syria and their opposition to other international military "interventions" (except, of course, for their own in Crimea and Georgia).

## Syria: The Arab Spring UNsprung

In Syria, the Arab Spring lost what little bounce it had. The government imprisoned and killed protesters, the opposition forces early on started bringing in weapons and armed men from other countries (which had never happened during the original Arab Spring, in Egypt), and a brutal and protracted civil war soon set in.

In the Security Council, there was never any agreement on how to respond. From late spring of 2011 on, the United States, United

Kingdom, and France were all openly and loudly advocating the overthrow of President Bashar al-Asad's government, while Russia and China were equally determined not to let that happen. In the absence of any consensus among the P5, Kofi Annan stepped in as a negotiator.

But soon enough Annan gave up, as did the man who succeeded him as the "special representative" of both the UN and the Arab League, Lakhdar Brahimi.

Syria's large northern neighbor, the NATO member Turkey, was a strong supporter of regime change, as were the Gulf Arab states. Turkey and the Gulf states poured large amounts of weapons to their allies in Syria, favoring Islamist rebels associated with Al-Qaeda over the more secular ones whom the CIA and later also the Pentagon were trying to support. One of the opposition formations favored by Washington was led by Syrian-Kurdish fighters ... but the Turks feared and hated the Kurds so much that they regularly bombed them. And rival militias supported by the CIA and the Pentagon even on occasion fought against each other. Go figure.

Russia and Iran meanwhile gave fairly steady military support to Asad, and Russia and China vetoed attempts to involve the ICC in Syria (which is not a party to it anyway), and also to investigate reports of nerve gas being used by the regime.

With conflicts and sub-conflicts raging throughout Syria, millions of Syrians became displaced inside and outside the country. The UN's High Commission on Refugees provided some support to those who left Syria, while a patchwork of UN and other aid bodies tries to help the ones displaced inside the country.

In Syria, as in so many earlier conflicts, the traumas suffered by the war's victims led to the rise of anti-humane extremism—in this case, the emergence of the Islamic State, ISIS. ISIS was incubated and established its base mainly in the regions along both sides of Syria's border with Iraq, a country that had suffered many of its own traumas in the aftermath of the United States's 2003 invasion.

With so many international actors involved in the war in Syria, it should have been a natural candidate for wise Security Council action, but the fractious and unpredictable state of the major powers was reflected in their collective ineffectiveness in Syria.

# SECTION 5
# The UN Alphabet

While the headlines mostly cover UN involvement in conflicts, the media usually underplay the huge amount of coordination and aid that the UN's component organizations do. A host of agencies and programs with varying degrees of independence and with over 200,000 staff work on boring, peaceful, and constructive projects. From the depths of the seabed to outer space, human life depends on countries agreeing on rules and coordination: about where ships can sail, planes fly, and satellites orbit. Perhaps because it generally works so well, this coordination work only gets noticed when it fails or there is controversy.

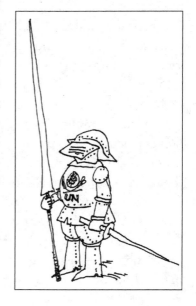

There is a UN heraldry. Just as medieval knights each had their own coat of arms, it seems the first thing a UN agency or office does is rush out and design its own distinctive logo. This makes the backdrop of UN conferences look like a medieval banqueting hall with all the shields on the wall!

The UN's agencies are very jealous of their symbols, guarding the copyright to them, and the UN's own name, flag, and logo are protected by international law—as the company that tried to set up a "UN Spy Shop" near UN headquarters in New York soon discovered. Indeed, in a global organization, a logo is worth a thousand words . . . just as long as people know what it means!

## So, Is the UN a System?

In 1947, an enthusiastic Belgian delegate described the UN as "a new system of a planetary type: a central organization, the United Nations, around which gravitated independent agencies linked with the former by special agreements." Sometimes it seems some of the agencies are in an orbit of their own! People try to diagram the structure, but the results look like a Jackson Pollack action painting.

Most bureaucracies, private and public, have only one government to worry about. The UN Secretariat has almost 200 of them to interfere and 70 years of sometimes contradictory instructions to implement, and that is before we get to more than 30 agencies and programs! There really is not much that's systematic about "The UN System."

Take tobacco. The WHO warns against smoking, while the FAO advises tobacco farmers on how to grow more of it, and GATT, the forerunner of the World Trade Organization (WTO) was very worried about governments that banned cigarette advertising. And ICAO, meanwhile, was working with the WHO to stop smoking on flights . . .

Originally, all the agencies were supposed to be under the UN Secretariat's close control. However, political pressures from member states allowed the various agencies to site themselves in faraway places and extenuate the lines of control and coordination. All the agencies sign Relationship Agreements with the UN, although the IMF, WTO, and World Bank agreements are somewhat one sided—almost representation without taxation!

While the US Congress has always complained about UN waste and duplication, it's usually a case of "do as I say, not as I do." Because President John F. Kennedy did not like the administrator of the Food and Agricultural Organization (FAO), Binay Ranjan Sen, the United States boosted the World Food Programme instead as a way to help dispose of US agricultural surpluses. Later, as part of another UN-related food fight, Henry Kissinger encouraged the establishment of a World Food Council.

Agency heads are separately appointed and want to do their own thing regardless, while the secretary-general has a hard enough time running the secretariat at home without trying to run the rest of the UN agencies. Even so, Boutros Boutros-Ghali, Kofi Annan, and Ban Ki-moon all tried to harmonize the work of the different agencies.

Annan even proposed to merge all the UN's development agencies into one body, but the agency heads soon shot down that proposal. They then reluctantly agreed to be part of the much looser UN Development Group (UNDG), which was set up in 1997 and tries to coordinate more than thirty constituent agencies and programs. (The Washington, DC-based World Bank, staunchly independent, is an observer rather than a member of it.)

The task of shepherding this herd of cats now falls to the United Nations System Chief Executives Board for Coordination (UNCEB), which has three supporting bodies: the High-level Committee on Programmes (HLCP), the High-level Committee on Management (HLCM), and that same old United Nations Development Group (UNDG).

Are you asleep yet?

These bodies' wordy names do not augur well—not least because in the UN, "High Level" all too often means "up in the air!"

In recent years, the coordination of UN bodies "in the field" (as UN insiders call the world outside HQ) has been somewhat improved by naming lead agencies for different sectors, and under pressure in some countries, "UN Houses" have brought most of the agencies under one roof to share facilities and accept common accounting standards. This "One UN" focus has improved communications among agencies and programs, reducing some duplication. But it is a never-ending task, trying to overcome organizational jealousy.

What makes it worse is that the UN doesn't have that much money for assistance: less than a dollar a year per head of the world's population. And to make it worse still, for every dollar the UN gives to the developing world, the World Bank extracts $1.20 back in interest charges on the "development" loans it has made!

A lot of people around the world welcomed António Guterres when he took office as secretary-general in 2017 because he had earlier run the refugee agency, UNHCR, a body that bypasses bureaucracy very effectively. They were especially heartened when in his first speech in the UN he told staff with feeling: "We need to try to get rid of this straitjacket of bureaucracy that makes our lives so difficult in many of the things we do."

# ■ UNLEASHING DEVELOPMENT AND HEALTH?

## Wealthy-World Organizations

Article 55 of the UN Charter calls for the promotion of worldwide full employment and the coordination of national full employment policies. But in 1944, at the same time the Western allies were planning for the future UN, they were also setting up the World Bank (formally called the International Bank for Reconstruction and Development) and the International Monetary Fund (IMF). They did this at a conference in Bretton Woods, New Hampshire. These are often called the Bretton Woods institutions.

At the UN, the voting rule is one country, one vote. But at these big global finance bodies, Wall Street rules apply: one vote per share. So the US dominates.

The Bretton Woods institutions have all the privileges of being part of the UN system but none of the accountability. The World Bank repudiated any binding coordination with the UN, refused to pledge delivery of information, limited secretariat attendance at its meetings, and insisted that the UN had no involvement in its budgets. But it attends UN meetings when it pleases.

Despite the Charter's Article 55, which proclaims the UN's commitment to promoting full employment, the IMF and World Bank have often made creating *unemployment* a condition of help. From the 1970s onward, they pioneered "Structural Adjustment Programs" that trashed developing economies by imposing neoliberal economic policies on them. Food subsidies and expenditures on health and education were cut along with wages, all in the name of productivity.

LITTLE RED RIDING HOOD UPDATED.....

In return for loans, the Bretton Woods gang insist that countries sell public assets cheaply, and they pushed for the convertibility of currencies and free trade—which all too often meant a gift to speculators and the destruction of local industries by large foreign competitors.

Many of the loans governments secured in return for impoverishing their own people only paid interest on existing debt and made no money available to fund new projects. Or it would end up in the private Swiss bank accounts of corrupt local officials. When it came time to repay the loans, it was the already hungry who had to tighten their belts.

In 1960, the richest 20 percent of the world's people earned 30 times the income of the other 80 percent. By 1989, they took sixty times. By 2015, 1 percent of the world's people owned half of its entire wealth.

Showing the power of faith, the IMF and World Bank, now joined by the European Union, persist in prescribing the same medicine, despite its repeated failures. In the real world, meanwhile, the so-called "Asian Tiger" economies all roared ahead precisely by *breaking* the World Bank's rules.

## The Better Bits

While the Bretton Woods institutions specialize in producing disasters and causing mass poverty, luckily parts of the UN *do* fight poverty, ill health, and underdevelopment and help to build a global society.

At the core of the UN's development efforts is the United Nations Development Programme (UNDP), which began as the Expanded Programme of Technical Assistance in 1950 when fifty-four nations pledged $20 million to it in multilateral aid. UNDP prides itself on being the biggest global multilateral aid-granting body and operates throughout the developing world, advising governments and other donors on integrated development planning.

The US monopolized the right to appoint the heads of UNDP and of the UN Children's Fund (UNICEF) for several decades. Indeed, jobs like that became part of the US presidential spoils system, and the

"AROUND HERE YOU'VE GOT TO WATCH OUT FOR THE MOSQUITOS THE WATER BORNE DISEASES AND, OF COURSE, THE ADULTS..."

lucky winners would have to leave when their patron quit the White House.

Of course, the rules of the UN absolutely forbid any such national allocation of posts! But to be fair, the appointees have often "gone native" and adopted a strong pro-UN attitude, defending their agencies against Congress. Anyway, under Kofi Annan, UNDP stopped being an "American job," and it has stayed that way—perhaps because Washington did not care about it anymore.

## The Human Development Report

Perhaps the biggest boost that UNDP gave to development was not financial or economic, but philosophical. UNDP turned the tide of development in 1990 when it published the first of its annual Human Development Reports. UNDP was headed by a US Republican appointee at the time, but the HDRs starkly challenged the orthodox neoliberal economics from the era of Ronald Reagan and Margaret Thatcher

that had been causing more devastation to developing countries than war and famine combined.

Until then, economic success was measured solely in money. For the IMF, World Bank, and Western governments, size mattered. Indeed, the size of a country's GDP was *all* that mattered.

To produce the HDRs, UNDP's researchers developed sophisticated assessments of human progress and aggregated them into a Human Development Index that indicates the overall health, education, and living standards of a country's people. Every year, the new edition of the HDR updates the index, while also examining one aspect of Human Development in greater depth. Like sports scores, the country rankings hit the headlines each year. They spread the word that development is about people, not just money! They contradict the IMF's bleak vision of the world, and they even seem to have converted many of the World Bank's people to their viewpoint.

The Index paved the way for the Millennium Development Goals, which were adopted by all the world's leaders in 2000.

To spur everyone's efforts, there were numerical targets to be reached by 2015. The idea of "league tables" for countries based on the scoring targets roused enthusiasm, and the whole project proved

The eight MDGs were:

1. Eradicate extreme poverty and hunger.
2. Achieve universal primary education.
3. Promote gender equality and empower women.
4. Reduce child mortality.
5. Improve maternal health.
6. Combat HIV/AIDS, malaria, and other diseases.
7. Ensure environmental sustainability.
8. Develop a global partnership for development.

remarkably effective. Despite the economic crisis of 2008, the world succeeded in rescuing millions of people from poverty and reducing mortality for mothers and children.

In 2016, UN members adopted a new set of targets, called the Sustainable Development Goals. The SDGs consist of 17 goals, subdivided into no fewer than 169 targets. UNDP describes the SDGs as "a universal call to action to end poverty, protect the planet, and ensure that all people enjoy peace and prosperity," adding that going beyond the MDGs they now also cover "new areas such as climate change, economic inequality, innovation, sustainable consumption, peace, and justice, among other priorities. The goals are interconnected—often the key to success on one will involve tackling issues more commonly associated with another."

## Knock Knock, WHO's There?

The World Health Organization (WHO) began in July 1946 as an interim commission, becoming an official agency on World Health Day, April 7, 1948. Since then, it has been much more successful at eradicating the scourge of diseases like smallpox than the UN has been at stopping the scourge of war.

In 1967, WHO set a target for the elimination of smallpox, and ten years later a team moved in on the Somali village of Merca where the last case of naturally occurring smallpox was reported. They inoculated

# The UN's Sustainable Development Goals, 2016

1. End poverty in all its forms everywhere.
2. End hunger, achieve food security and improved nutrition, and promote sustainable agriculture.
3. Ensure healthy lives and promote well-being for all at all ages.
4. Ensure inclusive and equitable quality education and promote lifelong learning opportunities for all.
5. Achieve gender equality and empower all women and girls.
6. Ensure availability and sustainable management of water and sanitation for all.
7. Ensure access to affordable, reliable, sustainable, and modern energy for all.
8. Promote sustained, inclusive, and sustainable economic growth, full and productive employment, and decent work for all.
9. Build resilient infrastructure, promote inclusive and sustainable industrialization, and foster innovation.
10. Reduce inequality within and among countries.
11. Make cities and human settlements inclusive, safe, resilient, and sustainable.
12. Ensure sustainable consumption and production patterns.
13. Take urgent action to combat climate change and its impacts.
14. Conserve and sustainably use the oceans, seas, and marine resources for sustainable development.
15. Protect, restore, and promote sustainable use of terrestrial ecosystems, sustainably manage forests, combat desertification, and halt and reverse land degradation and halt biodiversity loss.
16. Promote peaceful and inclusive societies for sustainable development, provide access to justice for all, and build effective, accountable, and inclusive institutions at all levels.
17. Strengthen the means of implementation and revitalize the global partnership for sustainable development.

the inhabitants and after a year in October 1979 yet another species, the smallpox virus, was declared extinct—without the usual protests!

The next target, set in 1988, was the elimination of polio by the year 2000. By 2014, it had reduced cases by 99 percent, but there are still pockets of the disease.

Malaria is a tougher challenge. It still kills 430,000 people a year, mostly babies and young children in sub-Saharan Africa, but between 2000 and 2015 the global anti-malaria initiative did cut the toll by 62 percent, and it looks as if there will soon be an effective vaccine against this ancient scourge.

The WHO has had less success with tuberculosis, but its international child immunization campaigns helped many countries to meet the Millennium Development Goals. Indeed, there are better child immunization rates in many developing countries than in the United States, and both maternal and infant mortality rates are plummeting across the developing world.

The WHO has helped to establish a "global health service" that puts investment into treatments that do not make much money commercially but that save lives, like its work on Ebola or malaria. Even the most selfish or insouciant Westerners now realize that with the pace and scale of modern travel, they can't close their eyes to diseases in other countries.

## UNAIDS

The best example of that was HIV/AIDS. Seeming to come out of nowhere in the 1980s, by the following decade AIDS was not just killing millions of people, it was on the verge of destroying entire vulnerable societies.

Now based in Geneva, UNAIDS was set up in 1994 to pull together governments, NGOs, and no less than ten relevant UN agencies to combat AIDS. Even the International Labour Organization (ILO), part of this coalition, is working to combat workplace discrimination against people with HIV.

Popularizing preventive methods played a large part, but the breakthrough needed science, law, and politics to work together to make treatment accessible. When the Millennium Development Goals finished in 2015, it still cost $10,000 a year for anti-retroviral treatments, so fewer than a million Africans could be treated. But UNAIDS and others challenged the claims big corporations made to intellectual property and licensing rights and brought the cost down to $100 a year. Now, over ten million people in sub-Saharan Africa are being treated.

## UNICEF

The United Nations Children's Emergency Fund (UNICEF) was created by the General Assembly in 1946 "to help protect the lives of children and promote their development." All these years later, far too many children around the world are still living through one emergency or another.

UNICEF's child immunization campaigns, allied with the WHO, have slashed infant mortality rates in many parts of the world. UNICEF works in many different ways to try to bolster children's health and wellbeing. It has even developed a "school in a box" that provides all the materials that a teacher would need to provide a basic education to up to forty children in a war-torn place like Afghanistan or Syria.

UNICEF is rare among agencies because it raises money directly from ordinary people in many countries, using mechanisms like its famous orange "trick or treat for UNICEF" boxes, or the sale of its famous greeting cards.

Many countries have national committees that channel donations to UNICEF. It is easier to raise money for mothers and children than for almost anything else. The rest of UNICEF's money comes from contributions from member states, which, although they may find it popular to cut foreign aid, find cutting funds to children is politically difficult—almost as hard as cutting arms purchases.

# UNFPA and UN Women

The United Nations Fund for Population Activities began with that name in the 1960s, funding population-related activities. Lots of people think the "FP" stands for family planning, not least because it does a lot of it! In 1987, it was officially renamed the United Nations Population Fund, but it kept the acronym UNFPA. Across the developing world, it helps countries provide sexual and reproductive health services, including family planning, especially to women and young people.

Birth control attracts controversy and has often had a strong ecumenical effect. Hardline Muslims, Protestants, Catholics, and even communists who see population control as an imperialist plot monitor UNFPA's work carefully. For its part, UNFPA always makes sure it offers a full range of reproductive health services, in addition to offering women the ability to choose whether and when to become pregnant.

UNFPA also works against female genital mutilation, in which campaign they are joined by UN Women, the agency that's the successor to the organization previously known as UNIFEM. (We told you this wouldn't be easy to understand.)

UN Women was formed when Ban Ki-moon tidied up a scattering of overlapping agencies to bring together the UN's work for social, economic, and legal equality for women into one agency. UN Women did not succeed in securing a female successor to him. But it did help to ensure that women's issues are prominent in the Sustainable Development Goals.

Even so, its head, South Africa's former Deputy President Phumzile Mlambo-Ngcuka, felt the need to point out in 2017 that only three of the seventy-one people who had served as President of the General Assembly were women—and, of course, zero of the nine SGs.

"Equality is not a statistic. It is a mindset," she declared as the UN has launched a campaign to achieve 50/50 gender party in all walks of life by 2030. She cited a study showing that only five out of thirty-five UN entities had reached the 50/50. Unsurprisingly, her own organization had made it to 78.9 percent.

## ■ UNEDUCATED? CALL UNESCO!

The United Nations Educational, Scientific and Cultural Organization (UNESCO) was established in response to a call from Arkansas Senator William Fulbright, a staunch internationalist who also set up the international scholarship program that bears his name despite representing a deeply segregationist southern state.

In the United States, UNESCO has always been a lightning rod for eccentric UN-haters. In the 1980s and 1990s, the excuse was Third World calls for a New World Information Order that would lessen the world's dependence on Western news sources. Later in the 1990s, the criticisms focused on UNESCO's program to designate World Heritage Sites, which were presented by the UN-haters as some form of UN land-grab. (At least one such campaign was funded by mining companies who objected to being told they could not mine right up to the boundaries of National Parks designated as heritage sites.)

Most countries fight to have their treasures enrolled as World Heritage Sites. For example, UNESCO helped save the ancient Egyptian temples at Abu Simbel from the Nile River waters rising behind the Aswan High Dam.

Ironically, it was under the most actively pro-UN of presidents, Barack Obama, that the United States lost its vote at UNESCO in 2013. That happened after Congress withheld US dues from the body after Palestine became a member state.

The UN has sometimes been called an example of the blind leading the blind. On at least one occasion, UNESCO put some truth into these rumors: In the 1950s, it developed standardized Braille and Braille music notation for the blind.

# ■ UNDOING DISASTERS

## The Office for Coordination of Humanitarian Affairs (OCHA)

The UN set up the Department of Humanitarian Affairs (OCHA) in 1991. It coordinated relief agencies and was allocated a revolving fund so there was cash for quick responses. Before that, the UN had to appeal and wait for donors to give, but the new fund allowed it to get its show on the road quickly without waiting for the donations to come in. However, the first appointee to head OCHA found that the agencies were uncooperative and the funds went only one way—quickly—while the SG of the time seemed pretty unapproachable. That appointee didn't stay for long.

Since then, OCHA has come into its own, coordinating UN agencies and government departments and even non-governmental organizations (NGOs). It rose to the occasion during the Asian tsunami of 2004 that killed 230,000 people. OCHA's work keeps expanding, not least since it often coordinates efforts by other national and non-profit agencies in major disasters.

## The World Food Programme (WFP)

Often the emergency food supplies that OCHA and its affiliated agencies use come from WFP, which feeds millions despite its politically charged history. It was set up in 1961 because the US did not like the head of the Food and Agriculture Organization! Its directors have a tendency to be close to the current US president, and it's sometimes criticized because while it does feed the starving, it generally uses US agriculture surpluses rather than cash or agricultural products from other countries to do so.

## UNHCR, for Refugees

The UN Convention on the Status of Refugees came into force in 1951, but the UN High Commission for Refugees had begun a year earlier with a three-year mandate to cope with the continuing aftermath of World War II.

Sadly, the refugees kept coming, and the twenty-first century has seen even more, with some now fleeing from the effects of climate change as well as from conflict. Technically, displaced people have to cross an international border to become designated as "refugees." If they remain inside their own country they are Internally

Displaced Persons (IDPs). UNHCR now intervenes for them as well, which is another reason its budget is now over twice the UN's own. Funded mostly by emergency grants, UNHCR also raises money from appeals to the public.

Around the globe, perilous seas and closed borders greet many of the people fleeing poverty, persecution, and conflict. UNHCR tries to temper the xenophobic reactions of many of the refugee-receiving governments.

UNHCR's former director, António Guterres, became the UN Secretary-General in January 2017.

## The United Nations Relief and Works Agency (UNRWA)

UNHCR's remit does not cover one of the longest-suffering groups of refugees: the Palestinians who in 1948–49 fled or were expelled from the area that became Israel, who have never been allowed to return to their homes. They and their descendants are helped instead by

UNRWA, whose full name is the UN Relief and Works Agency for Palestine Refugees in the Near East.

Because of the UN's own role in partitioning Palestine, the Assembly clearly felt responsibility for the refugees that decision had helped to create. In its Resolution 194 of 1948, the Assembly specifically determined that in the context of a final peace settlement these refugees had the right to return to their homes or be compensated for the property they had left behind. In the meantime, the UN would help look after them. In the nearly seventy years since, there has been no final peace settlement.

Today, UNRWA provides food, education, and health care to some five million Palestinian refugees. It has also provided jobs for many of them. Only around a hundred of them are official UN staff, but UNRWA is the UN's biggest agency, with over 30,000 employees.

The Agency educates almost half a million students in its schools and provides three million Palestinians with healthcare. Partly as a result of UNRWA's work, Palestinians have the highest education levels of any country in the Arab world.

As with anything to do with the Palestinians and Israelis, UNRWA is always controversial. Israeli governments are happy that the UN pays for many of the services that the Geneva Conventions say the occupiers should provide in occupied territories. But pro-Israeli politicians in the US Congress often attack it and threaten its funding. Until the Palestinian-Israeli conflict is finally resolved, however, UNRWA will stay around.

# ■ THE ENVIRONMENT: NOT JUST HOT AIR!

One of the many reasons some conservatives dislike the United Nations is that it keeps putting climate change on the world agenda. In fact, that is not quite true. It's *reality* that keeps putting it on the agenda, what with shrinking ice caps, rising sea levels, and more storms than ever.

Carbon dioxide knows no boundaries; even the highest border fence won't stop smog, and customs officers can't impound tsunamis. While oil and coal lobbyists can pressure the US Congress into ignoring climate change, they are less successful with the UN—although they certainly try!

In 1972, the United Nations Environment Programme (UNEP) began its work, following the holding of a key environmental conference in Stockholm, Sweden. Since then, UNEP has been the catalyst for several significant international agreements.

The "environment" covers almost everything humanity does, and UNEP has innumerable panels and conventions working on different aspects of its task. One of its earliest achievements was the Convention on the International Trade in Endangered Species of Wild Fauna and Flora (CITES). CITES has several achievements, among them the ban on the international ivory trade, which has greatly reduced the slaughter of elephants (although poaching still continues).

In 1988, UNEP joined with the World Meteorological Organization to set up the Intergovernmental Panel on Climate Change (IPCC), endorsed by the General Assembly. IPCC's regular and measured reports on the effects of greenhouse gases send fossil-fuel advocates into paroxysms of rage and denial.

The IPCC's calmly presented assessments of the evidence and its conclusions have convinced most governments that climate change is a real threat and is caused by humans. But there are still many governments and corporations that don't want science to interfere with moneymaking activities like selling carbon-based

fuels. Its 2007 report that proved the reality of global warming earned it a Nobel Prize—but also the rage of pseudo-scientists and fuel lobbyists all around the world.

In recent years, the UN's Framework Convention on Climate Change (UNFCCC) has become the crucial global body for trying to control the emissions of $CO_2$ and other harmful gases. We know it can be done. In the 1980s, when industrialized countries saw the effects of the disappearing ozone layer and the resulting threats of cancer to their own citizens, they quickly agreed to the Montreal Protocol, which phased out production of the refrigerant chemicals (CFCs) that were responsible.

Kofi Annan called the Montreal Protocol "perhaps the single most successful international agreement to date." It rapidly stabilized and is now gradually restoring the ozone layer. One of the secrets is that the ozone hole was spreading from the poles—threatening higher skin cancer rates in the temperate developing world—and cynics contrasted

> If we took away barriers to women's leadership, we would solve the climate change problem a lot faster.
> **Mary Robinson**

## Nation Shall Talk unto Nation—But It's Hard Work

It might not be a global *government* as feared by the isolationists in the US, but it was definitely the need for global *governance* that led to the establishment of many of the multinational agencies now tied to the UN. If you want letters, telephones, telegrams, or even emails and airplanes to go from one country to another, then all concerned have to agree to common standards . . .

this with indifference to the plight of tropical islanders drowning because of global warming.

But soon, scientists worldwide realized the refrigerant chemicals used to substitute for CFCs to combat ozone depletion, HFCs, were a very serious cause of global warming—worse than $CO_2$. So at another UN-sponsored conference held in Kigali, Rwanda, in October 2016, governments agreed to strengthen the controls on HFCs.

But greenhouse gas emissions are much more difficult to rein in. Nearly everyone in the world burns fuels, whether wood, coal, petroleum, or diesel. Pollution in countries such as China and India and the visible effects of climate change, whether from drought or flooding, have persuaded even previously skeptical governments that the threat is real. But it's an uphill struggle to get humanity to give up fossil fuels. There's money in them thar smokestacks.

The big UN climate-change conferences held around the world—from Kyoto to Copenhagen to Paris—have seen a diplomatic war of attrition with inadequate targets being set and then missed. The 2015 Paris Agreement on emission reduction was actually legally binding, though President Trump has tried to find a way to wriggle out of it. But it is still woefully unequal to the challenge.

Global warming is like nuclear war: The UN has to try to save the world from it! There is no alternative organization that can do it.

# The Stamp of Success—
# Philately Gets You Everywhere!

In 1947, the Argentinian President of the General Assembly, Dr. José Arce, a stamp collector, suggested that the UN issue its own stamps. The Assembly agreed, and in 1951 the UN issued its first stamps. The agreement with the US Post Office Department specified that the UN's stamps had to be in US currency and used only at the New York HQ. Later, the UN reached similar agreements with the governments hosting its large centers in Geneva, Switzerland (1968) and Vienna, Austria (1979).

The motivation was prestige, since it made the UN the first intergovernmental agency to issue stamps, propaganda for the UN message—and revenue, since stamp collectors have avidly bought hundreds of UN stamp issues.

The first UN commemorative stamps were issued by the (stamp-sized) republic of San Marino, which only joined the UN in 1992!

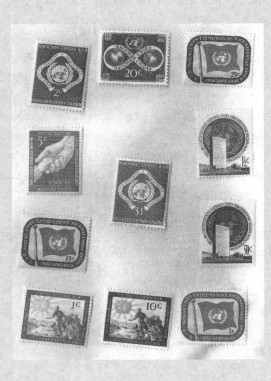

# ■ THE UN'S OTHER TECHNICAL AGENCIES

## The Universal Postal Union (UPU)—The Stamp of Approval

In 1863, US Postmaster General Montgomery Blair took time out from the Civil War to propose the international coordination of mail deliveries. It was an odd time to go for globalization!

After frank talks, the UPU was set up in 1875 to sort out how mail crossed borders. It was a sort of paper internet. In general, national post offices agreed that they would all deliver foreign mail without charging the originating country. Each kept the revenue from the stamps they sold.

Because Britain invented stamps, it does not have to put its name on the stamps it issues, as long as they show the monarch's head. (If Britain ever becomes a republic, this could change.)

Based in Bern, Switzerland, the UPU became a specialized agency of the UN in 1948. It was also the backdoor through which the postage-stamp-sized Vatican City became a genuine postage-stamp state when it was allowed to join the UPU and thus gained some acceptance by a UN agency. You could say that philately gets you everywhere!

## More About Communications

In the nineteenth century, globalization already demanded universal standards. In a world of telegraphs, trains, and ocean voyages, it was essential we all knew where and when we were! In 1884, most countries agreed that maps and clocks should count from the Greenwich, thenceforth the prime, meridian, a north-south line that goes through the British Royal Observatory near London.

The world's clocks are set by the UN-affiliated International Astronomical Union (IAU), in conjunction with the International Telecommunications Union (ITU). The ITU was originally established in 1865 in Paris as the International Telegraph Union to coordinate standards and charges for the then-new technology of telegraphy, which was the sending of text messages over long distances using only electric wires.

One key international standard established by the ITU was the Morse code, a way of telegraphing letters and numbers into a series of dots and dashes, which was developed by American artist and inventor Samuel F.B. Morse.

Soon thereafter, the ITU branched out into creating international standards for telephones, and in 1932 it began to allocate radio bandwidths.

Even now, American astronauts, Russian cosmonauts, and space explorers from other nations coordinate their work together by using Greenwich Mean Time, and the ITU still divvies up the use of the electromagnetic spectrum between different countries.

The Internet Corporation for Assigned Names and Numbers (ICANN), the body that has regulated the use of its top-level domain names since the dawn of the Internet, is not itself a UN affiliate. But UN agencies such as UNESCO, WHO, ITU, and the UPU are "observers" on ICANN's Governmental Advisory Committee.

# Tonga: The Mouse That Went Orbital

Satellites orbiting 22,300 miles up around the equator always remain in the same position in relation to the ground. There are only a limited number of such Geo-Stationary Orbit (GSO) slots, and in 1994 Ecuador wanted the UN to recognize the special relationship between the slots and the equatorial countries. (*Ecuador* is Spanish for "equator"!)

Russia recommended that the geosynchronous orbit should be part of the "Common Heritage of Mankind" like the seabed. Needless to say, Russia leans more towards the Arctic than the Equator.

The small country of Tonga has a population of some 100,000, with one port, one airport, no railroads, and 283 miles of roads. But it's located near the Equator, in the middle of the mostly empty Pacific, and in 1988, it put in a bid for the sixteen of the GSO slots left unclaimed.

There was outrage from many other countries, but Tonga still ended up with six slots. There was some question about whether the slots belonged to the country or to the princess whose company got its hands on them and then leased them to international companies that were (unlike Tonga itself) actually able to send up satellites to occupy them.

# The International Civil Aviation Organization (ICAO)

During the First World War, the pace of life had sped up. Airplanes had moved from being scientific toys to major means of warfare and transport. Swords might not yet have been converted to plowshares, but after the end of World War I many bombers were converted to cargo and passenger planes. In 1919, at the Paris Peace Conference, a special Aeronautical Commission was established that in turn led to the creation of a new International Commission for Air Navigation, which in 1947 became the International Civil Aviation Organization (ICAO).

Based in Montreal, the ICAO sets standards for aircraft safety and pilot training. Its agreements allow countries to accept each other's certification for planes and crew, and to set standards for airports, controllers, and all the other things you hope you can take for granted when you're flying along five miles above the ground.

# The International Maritime Organization (IMO)

Surprisingly (since, after all, boats came before planes), the Inter-Governmental Maritime Consultative Organization, now the IMO, did

not come together until 1948. It has been regulating maritime safety and environmental pollution ever since. It has serious work to do. Ships often burn the lowest, most polluting grades of oil and with fuel spillages and ballast dumping can do serious harm to the seas, the seabed, and coastal communities.

# The International Labour Organization (ILO)

When those ships are at sea, the sailors who work them get some protection from the ILO, whose many conventions include work codes for them . . .

Founded in 1919, the ILO is the only agency of the old League of Nations still in existence. Now in the UN system, it is supposed to have representatives of governments, unions, and employers and to set standards for working environments. It won the Nobel Peace Prize in 1969 for its work—"by means of a levering of income and a progressive policy of social welfare," the award announcement claimed, "the ILO has played its part . . . in bridging the gap between rich and poor."

ILO standards and reports still get overlooked in many countries. But it has helped millions of working people around the world to organize and to get paid properly for their work. That puts the ILO almost in direct opposition to the Bretton Woods institutions, which push for lower wages and less security for workers as the key to economic progress!

# SECTION 6
# The UN and the Future

Seventy years was once seen as a good lifespan for a person, and seventy-plus years is a good stretch for organizations as well. So, the big question for the UN now is whether it is fit for its purpose—and indeed, whether the purpose has changed since 1945.

The world has changed a lot since 1945, but many of the problems are still the same. Or bigger. The big problem they had just dealt with was conflicts between nation states, but just think: there are almost four times as many nation states to be quarrelsome now. And back then, only one of them had nuclear weapons. Now, we know of at least nine.

Now, too, more than ever before, there are non-state actors with very easy access to cheap weaponry. The AK-47 rifle in all its forms has killed more people than the atom bomb so far, and the UN's efforts to control the small-arms trade has not been very successful. It's true that, thanks to the UN's efforts, only nine countries have nukes, but almost all (including the United States) have more small arms than they can cope with.

Today, with globalization, economic and financial instability pose more of a threat than ever, as do the new diseases that mass air travel can so easily spread from continent to continent. And of course, climate change is completely border-free in its effects. It is some comfort that challenges such as these would be far larger and scarier without the UN to focus global efforts. But too much remains undone.

Like any seventy-year-old vehicle, the UN could do with an over-haul. But tinkering with the mechanism of a moving vehicle is not so easy—and it could distract from setting the right course.

Even so, let's look at some of the proposed reforms.

## ■ THE SECURITY COUNCIL: REFORM, PERHAPS?

The original UN Charter called for the members to decide whether to hold a Revision Convention in 1955. They didn't, and just increased the number of temporary Security Council members. Many members—then and now—have argued that the council makeup, especially the role and power of the P5, does not reflect the modern world.

The Assembly can alter the charter with a two-thirds vote, but even then, any one of the P5 can still veto any reform that would strip them of their vetoes!

In 1994, the Assembly set up the "Open-ended Working Group on the Question of Equitable Representation on and Increase in the Membership of the Security Council and Other Matters Related to the Security Council." Any committee with a title like that is *not* going to be in a rush. It is still meeting and wrangling.

France and Britain are protective of their permanent seats and resist suggestions that the European Union should replace them. Because they can veto any changes, most reform proposals keep Britain and France as permanent members (and Britain's decision in 2016 to leave the EU messed up the plan to replace those two P5 seats with a single EU one, anyway).

So most of the discussion about SC reform has been about *adding* new permanent members. But if Germany and Japan, who both pay more dues to the UN than Britain, France, and Russia, were to become permanent, that would tilt the balance against the developing world. As a result, many proposals have suggested adding Brazil, India, and either Nigeria, South Africa, or Egypt, as well. And they all want a veto of their very own!

The rivalry between all these potential "Permanent Seat" claimants has kept the issue unsolved for over twenty years. But it's hard to imagine that five more potential veto-wielders would make the Council more effective.

To match new permanent members, some reformers also want to add more non-permanent elected members. But adding ten more members would make the Council more like a mass rally than a decisive committee. Other suggestions have included adding five less temporary members, who would have longer terms and be able to stand for re-election. So, for example, India and Japan would have to be nice to their neighbors if they wanted to get re-elected.

In fact, reforming the Security Council is something that really only preoccupies diplomats whose idea of heaven is to sit on it! For the rest of us, it is far more important to have an *effective* Council that can actually act to avert threats and implement the UN Charter, although the perception of geographical imbalance does erode the perceived legitimacy of the UN's moral authority.

There have also been proposals to have NGOs represented at the UN, or even to have parliamentarians there in some form, or direct elections for representatives (as in the EU's parliament). But since so many of the UN's member governments don't allow elections at home, then global elections might lack some transparency and authenticity. And though it's true that many NGOs do great work, it is also true that any billionaire or right-wing/racist network can set up its own foundations, as US elections have demonstrated.

That does not mean, though, that "We, the peoples" have no role to play. Yes, the UN is an organization of governments—but it is an organization in which governments *have to show their real selves in public!* If the public and the press can overcome the yawn factor and keep track of what their governments say and do in the UN, they (we) can hold our representatives to task, and assess their actions by the standards they subscribed to in the UN Charter and its consequent conventions and resolutions.

In the end, however, it is up to the governments to act wisely. But without being unfair, currently it is one government above all, the

US government, whose contradictory principles and prejudices are reflected in the UN.

## ■ THE UNITED STATES AND THE UN

The United States set up the UN, and most presidents since 1945 have paid public lip-service to it and to the international legality it represents. But for half a century now, the State Department has had to educate the White House and fight off a Congress that does not accept that the US should take any notice of foreigners "telling them what to do"— even though most presidents and legislators have seemed happy to do the bidding of lobbyists for foreign powers that are unhappy with the UN's decisions. When the most powerful (not to mention the founding) member of the organization flouts international law whenever it wants, it does not really set a great example to the others.

The UN has often been a favorite target for America-Firsters. And lobbies on Israel, guns, or even on grazing rights on federal land near World Heritage sites, could always get a boost in their publicity and their fundraising by inventing a "fiendish" UN connection to their cause, no matter how spurious.

In 2015, however, the UN-haters in the United States seemed hardly to notice when, without much fanfare, President Barack Obama quietly overturned Clinton's Presidential Decisions Directive 25, which had been partly responsible for the UN's tacit connivance in the Rwanda genocide. (See pages 105–7.)

Obama's new directive now said that the United States

> has a compelling national security interest in preventing the outbreak, escalation, and spread of conflicts that could contribute to these threats, but we cannot and should not seek to assume that burden on our own. To the contrary, it is in our interest to strengthen international response mechanisms that enable the burden to be shared globally. Multilateral peace operations, particularly United Nations (UN) peace operations, will, therefore, continue to be among the primary international tools that we use to address conflict-related crises. . . .

To strengthen and modernize UN peace operations, US policy will continue to be to fulfill our treaty obligations to the UN by paying our assessed dues in full and on time.

However, that did not stop the Obama administration from carrying out congressional policy and withdrawing from UNESCO when that organization accepted Palestine as a member.

Then, in December 2016, the UN Security Council voted to condemn Israel's continued building of settlements in the Occupied Palestinian Territories in defiance of innumerable resolutions from both the General Assembly and the Security Council. On this occasion, for once, the United States did not veto the resolution, but abstained.

Congress once again called for withholding dues to the UN—to punish the organization for adopting a resolution that the US had not opposed and which the other fourteen members of the Security Council all supported!

It was an ominous moment for US-UN relations. However, while the United States is still undoubtedly an important actor at the UN, it is no longer uniquely essential for the organization's success. For example, China is now taking a much more active role than it used to, and contributing much more in dues and peacekeeping costs than it used to, making it the UN's second-biggest paying member after the US. That diminishes the power of the US Congress to micromanage UN policy. China is far from being a perfect global citizen. But when it signed onto UNFCCC's Paris Convention on Climate Change in 2015, that was a huge step forward, especially in contrast to promises by then-presidential candidate Trump to withdraw from it.

# ■ SO, IS IT ALL WORTHWHILE?

People have a whole spectrum of degrees of enthusiasm and cynicism about the UN. Real supporters of the UN are realists; they know its failings. (They don't have UNreal expectations.) Even many of those who were deeply involved in its creation curb their enthusiasm when assessing its achievements. The veteran British diplomat Sir Brian Urquhart was the UN's second employee—and he continued working

If anyone were to say China is playing a leadership role in the world I would say it's not China rushing to the front but rather the front runners have stepped back leaving the place to China.
**China's President Xi Jinping, January 2017**

In the face of an absolutely unprecedented emergency, society has no choice but to take dramatic action to avert a collapse of civilization. Either we will change our ways and build an entirely new kind of global society, or they will be changed for us.
**Gro Harlem Brundtland, three-term Prime Minister of Norway and former Director-General of the WHO**

there for forty years. He once said, fairly cautiously, "I'd rather regard the UN as a qualified success than an unqualified failure."

The UN can reform. It has evolved well beyond the victors' cabal of 1945. It invented peacekeeping, and it has built a whole support structure for international development and cooperation and for advancing human rights. With R2P it brought in a legal framework matching our common global responsibility for each other's survival. The very real challenges posed by climate change are inducing some hitherto unlikely nations to work together.

Which brings us back to where we started. The UN might not be perfect, and it could be better, but the price of reforming and replacing the League of Nations was heavy: the Second World War. . . . And the whole point and success of the UN so far has been to avoid World War Three.

Perhaps we can sum it up by quoting what Secretary General António Guterres said when he launched his campaign for the job in 2016:

> In times of insecurity, when people feel uncertain about their future, when anxieties and fears are promoted and exploited by political populists, old-fashioned nationalists, or religious fundamentalists, the success of the UN and the international community lies in our common commitment to our common values.

*New SG Antonio Guterres welcomes Nigeria's former Environment Minister, Amina Muhamed, as Deputy SG.*

# Somebody Loves the UN!

The UN's Nobel Prizes (all, except where noted, for contributions towards peace):

1945: Cordell Hull, US Secretary of State, for his work establishing the UN

1950: Ralph Bunche, for the Middle East

1954 and 1981: UNHCR

1961 Dag Hammarskjöld

1965: UNICEF

1969: ILO

1979: Abdus Salam of IAEA (for Physics)

1979: Sir Arthur Lewis of St. Lucia (for Economics), much of it for his work with UNDP on development

1989: UN peacekeeping forces

2001: The UN as a whole, jointly with Kofi Annan

2005: The IAEA, jointly with Mohamed ElBaradei

2007: IPCC, jointly with Al Gore Jr.

2013: OPCW

# ADDITIONAL RESOURCES

**National Model United Nations** | www.nmun.org

The Minneapolis-based National Collegiate Conference Association/ National Model United Nations (NCCA/NMUN) is a U.S. 501(c)(3) nonprofit organization that advances understanding of the United Nations and contemporary international issues among college and university students.

NMUN organizes a number of "Model UN" conferences annually that involve students as delegates representing all the UN's members. Its principle of cooperative, hands-on, experiential learning allows students to confront a range of topics with the perspective of their assigned country or organization. Through these experiences, students develop an appreciation of differing viewpoints, experience the challenges of negotiation, see the rewards of cooperation, broaden their world view, and discover the human side of international relations and diplomacy.

NCCA/NMUN has been a recognized Non-Governmental Organization (NGO) associated with the United Nations Department of Public Information (DPI) since 1982.

**The Hague International Model United Nations** | www.thimun.org

THIMUN is an international organization, based in The Hague (Netherlands), that organizes student-run Model UN conferences in several countries around the world. Its mission is to promote and foster collaborative solution-oriented discussion to important issues by instilling life-long passion for improving our global community into today's youth, who will be tomorrow's leaders.

THIMUN also runs an Online Model UN program for high-school students. Details are at onlinemodelunitednations.org/.

**World Federation of United Nations Associations** | wfuna.org

WFUNA, which has offices in New York, Seoul, Geneva, and Brussels, is a global nonprofit organization that unites the work of more than 100 nationally-based United Nations Associations around the world.

Guided by its vision of a United Nations that is a powerful force in meeting common global challenges and opportunities, WFUNA works to strengthen and improve the United Nations. It seeks to achieve this through the engagement of people who share a global mindset and support international cooperation—global citizens.

The U.S. affiliate of the WFUNA is the United States Association of the USA (http://www.unausa.org/), which is headquartered in Washington, DC and New York and has numerous chapters around the country.

# ACKNOWLEDGMENTS

We are grateful to all the people who helped and encouraged us to write this, not least Secretary General Ban Ki-moon who read *The UN for Beginners*, which was originally published in the United Kingdom in 1995, and suggested an updated rewrite!

Thanks and apologies to Ian's sons, Owain and Ian, who rewarded parental neglect by adding young perspectives to the book! In particular, we want to thank our other volunteer proofreaders, Carmen Johns, Mary Eliza Kimball, Marianne Kosits, Carlos Santos Tejada, and Amanda Schiacchitano; and the UN Department of Public Information, in particular USG Cristina Gallach and acting USG Maher Nasser for their cooperation in opening the UN Photo Archives.

And, of course, thanks to Just World Books' Helena Cobban and Marissa Wold Uhrina for their efforts to pull this book together on impossible deadlines!

~Ian & Krishna

# ABOUT THE AUTHOR
# AND ILLUSTRATOR

**Ian Williams** is a prolific writer who has been covering the United Nations since 1989. He has personally known four Secretaries General, and innumerable diplomats and officials worldwide. In 1995, for the fiftieth anniversary of the United Nations, while he was president of the UN Correspondents' Association, Williams wrote *UN for Beginners*, which provided a model for *UNtold*.

Born in Liverpool, UK, Williams played as a child in the rubble of bombsites left over from the war that inspired the founding of the United Nations. He hopes the UN will spare him from reporting on World War III.

Williams currently lectures at Bard's Center for Globalization and International Affairs, on the UN and the Responsibility to Protect. He has won awards for his exposés of UN malfeasance but is supportive of its mission and quick to defend it from detractors.

**Krishna** is the pen-name of a cartoonist whose work has appeared widely in the *Guardian* and elsewhere. He previously won awards from illustration work he did for "Sesame Street".